NETFLIX

STRANGER THINGS

ANNUAL 2026

STRANGER THINGS

CONTENTS

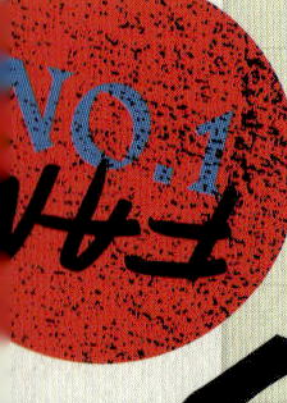

FOR WILL
STRANGER THINGS
PALACE
ARCADE
CAMP
KNOW WHERE
UPSIDE
DOWN

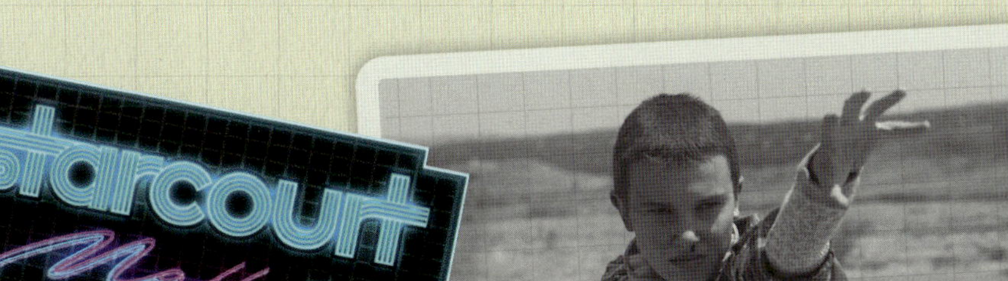
Starcourt

FUN FAIR
HELLFIRE CLUB
HELLFIRE CLUB
HELLFIRE CLUB

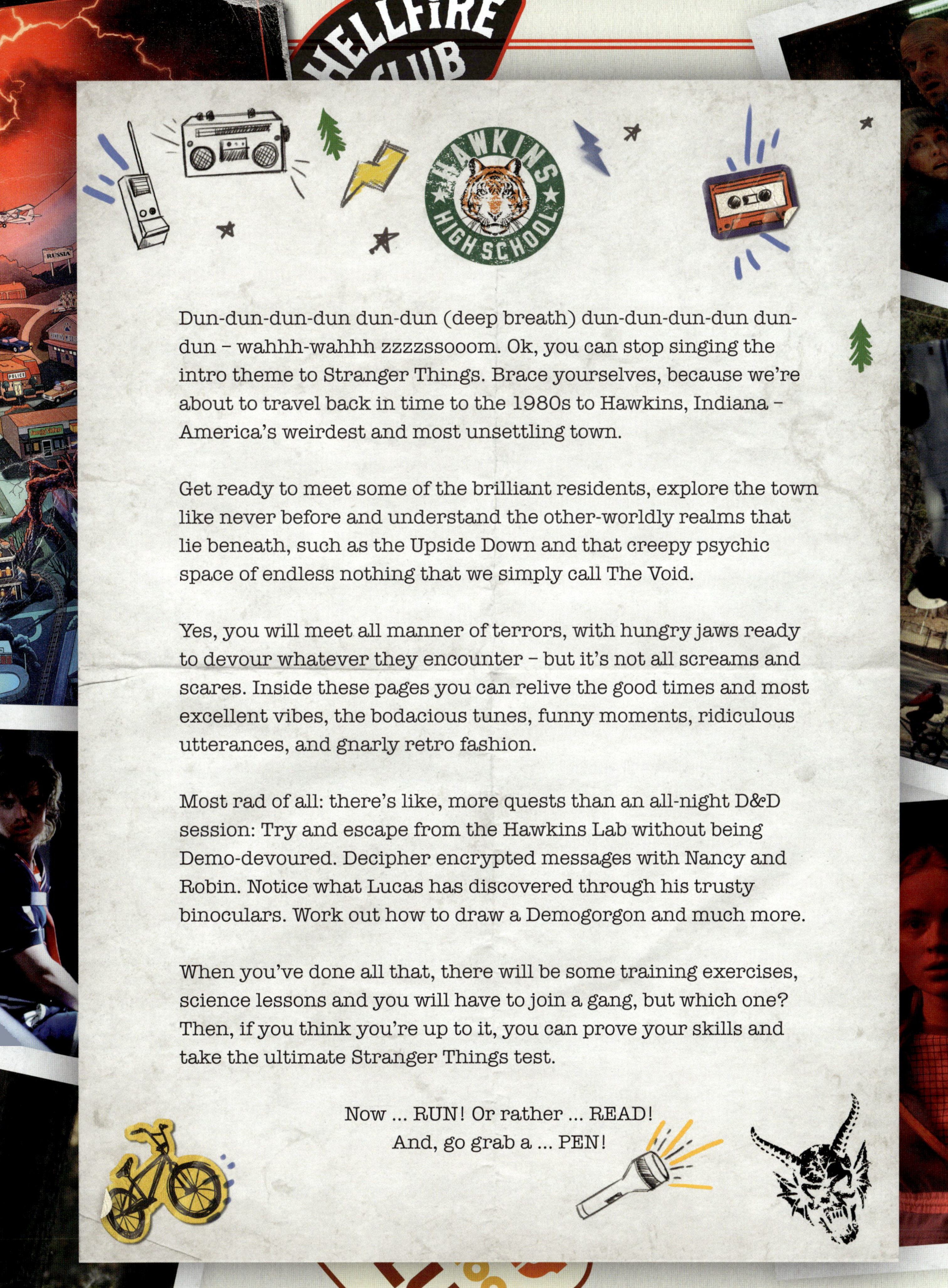

Dun-dun-dun-dun dun-dun (deep breath) dun-dun-dun-dun dun-dun – wahhh-wahhh zzzzssooom. Ok, you can stop singing the intro theme to Stranger Things. Brace yourselves, because we're about to travel back in time to the 1980s to Hawkins, Indiana – America's weirdest and most unsettling town.

Get ready to meet some of the brilliant residents, explore the town like never before and understand the other-worldly realms that lie beneath, such as the Upside Down and that creepy psychic space of endless nothing that we simply call The Void.

Yes, you will meet all manner of terrors, with hungry jaws ready to devour whatever they encounter – but it's not all screams and scares. Inside these pages you can relive the good times and most excellent vibes, the bodacious tunes, funny moments, ridiculous utterances, and gnarly retro fashion.

Most rad of all: there's like, more quests than an all-night D&D session: Try and escape from the Hawkins Lab without being Demo-devoured. Decipher encrypted messages with Nancy and Robin. Notice what Lucas has discovered through his trusty binoculars. Work out how to draw a Demogorgon and much more.

When you've done all that, there will be some training exercises, science lessons and you will have to join a gang, but which one? Then, if you think you're up to it, you can prove your skills and take the ultimate Stranger Things test.

Now ... RUN! Or rather ... READ!
And, go grab a ... PEN!

WELCOME TO HAWKINS

Hawkins is like many small towns in the Midwest, except with more demonic possessions and sudden deaths by interdimensional petal-heads.

You're very welcome in Hawkins. Stay alive as long as you can.

Hawkins has a long history of traditional values and old-fashioned small-town hospitality.

Reports of Satanic death cults have been over exaggerated.

Unlike most towns in America, there's a real camaraderie between the generations in Hawkins. There's nothing like fighting the forces of evil to bring a community together.

WELCOME TO HAWKINS

Testimonials from residents

"HAWKINS ... AT THE VERY BEST WE'RE A TOILET STOP ON YOUR WAY TO DISNEYLAND."
ROBIN BUCKLEY

"I'LL TELL YA, YOU START TO BELIEVE ALL THOSE THINGS THEY SAY: THAT THIS TOWN IS CURSED AND THAT THE DEVIL LIVES HERE IN HAWKINS."
UN-NAMED RESIDENT

"THE SHADOW MONSTER ... IT'S LIKE HE'S REACHING INTO HAWKINS MORE AND MORE."
WILL BYERS

"A CULT ... OPERATES RIGHT HERE IN HAWKINS."
JASON CARVER

"HAWKINS IS IN DANGER ... A WAR IS COMING TO HAWKINS."
DR SAM OWENS

"I SAW A DARK CLOUD SPREADING OVER HAWKINS. DOWNTOWN ON FIRE ... AND THIS GIANT CREATURE WITH ... A GAPING MOUTH."
NANCY WHEELER

Find Hawkins a zippy 80 miles from Indianapolis

HAWKINS POLICE
INDIANA

HAWKINS NATIONAL LABORATORY
U.S. DEPT OF ENERGY

LEAVING
HAWKINS
COME AGAIN SOON

11 HAWKINS HIGHWAYS AND BYWAYS, THIS WAY AND THAT

1. CORNWALLIS ROAD
2. DEARBORN
3. KERLEY
4. LOCH NORA
5. MAPLE STREET
6. MOREHEAD STREET
7. MULBERRY STREET
8. OAK HIGHWAY
9. OLIVE BRANCH ROAD
10. POPLAR TREE ROAD
11. RANDOLPH LANE

While Hawkins used to be a safe neighbourhood, these days parents and law-enforcement are baffled by the goings-on. Teenagers can be so secretive. A county-wide initiative to leave doors open three inches is being trialled. That'll help.

If you see this girl rob a convenience store or explode an Orange Julius smoothie in someone's face – allow it. Keep your trap shut and move on.

STRANGER TIMES

HAWKINS TIMELINE: PART 1

To keep track of what happened when and with who. The 'why' is much harder to answer.

1800s

■ The town of Hawkins is founded in Indiana, USA.

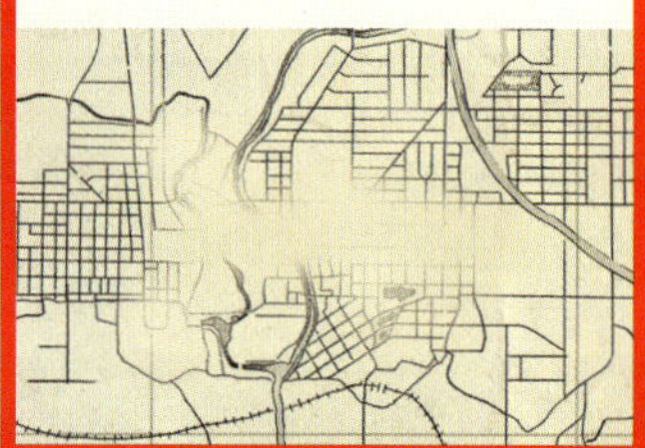

1943

■ The USS Eldridge, a US Navy vessel involved in secret experiments known as 'Project Rainbow' and the 'Philadelphia Experiment', goes missing, then it returns. Turns out that it had travelled to Dimension X.

Late 1940s

■ The sole survivor of the USS Eldridge's voyage to Dimension X was the father of Dr Martin Brenner, who tells his son everything on his deathbed.

1970

■ Jane Ives takes part in the experimental program MKUltra at Hawkins Lab.

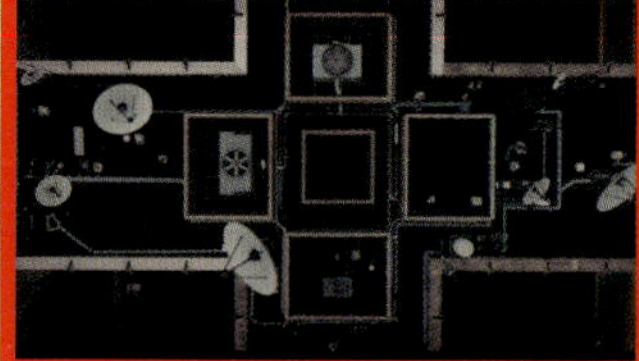

1971

■ Dustin, Mike, Will, Lucas and Max are born, and so is Eleven with her special telekenetic powers.

1973

■ The government officially abandons the MKUltra project.

1974

■ Terry Ives breaks into Hawkins Lab to rescue her daughter Jane – aka Eleven, but Terry is captured and given electric shocks, which put her in a catatonic state.

1975

■ Lucas' little sister, Erica, is born.

1976

■ Best friends, Mike and Will meet at kindergarten.

1978

■ Kalli aka subject 008 escapes from Hawkins Lab.

■ Chief Hopper's daughter Sarah is diagnosed with cancer and dies shortly after.

1950s

■ Dr Brenner tries to replicate the Philadelphia Experiment in Nevada, but someone steals his equipment, hiding it in a nearby cave.

■ A young boy, Henry Creel, finds the equipment in the cave and is transported to the other dimension, where he encounters the Mind Flayer. When he returns to our world he is utterly changed.

1953

■ Project MKUltra is given the go-ahead by the CIA. It was a government scheme that ran experiments on humans that often involved the use of harmful chemicals.

1959

■ The Creel family move into a massive Victorian mansion in Hawkins.

1960s

■ Henry Creel is taken to Hawkins National Laboratory to be studied by Dr Brenner. He is the first child subject. Code named: 001.

1967

■ Nancy, Jonathan, Billy and Barb are born.

1968

■ Robin is born.

1979

■ Henry Creel, aka 001, kills all the test subjects at the Hawkins National Laboratory, apart from Jane, aka 011, who opens a gate to another world, sending and trapping him there.

■ Hopper returns to his hometown and becomes Police Chief.

1980

■ Dustin Henderson moves to Hawkins and joins Will, Mike and Lucas' D&D group.

1983

■ Eleven accidentally reopens the gate to the alternate dimension, the Upside Down, and all hell breaks loose.

STRANGER TIMES

HAWKINS TIMELINE: PART 2

A lot can happen in four years ...

6 November 1983

- Eleven escapes from Hawkins Laboratory.
- Will Byers is abducted by the Demogorgon.

7 November 1983

- Searching for Will in the woods, Mike, Dustin and Lucas find a girl called Eleven instead. Mike takes her home and lets her stay the night.

8 November 1983

- Eleven reveals that Will is hiding in the Upside Down.
- Barb is the next victim of the Demogorgon.

9 November 1983

- Joyce Byers makes contact with Will in the Upside Down using a string of fairy lights. Will tells her to RUN – just before a Demogorgon breaks through the wall.

3 November 1984

- Eleven, who has been living a secret life in Hopper's cabin, hitchhikes to see her mother, who is in a trance-like state. She then travels to Chicago to meet her HNL 'sister' Kali, aka subject 008.
- Joyce's new boyfriend Bob Newby realises that drawings Will has been furiously creating under the influence of the Mind Flayer are a map of tunnels beneath Hawkins. They use these to find and rescue Hopper.

5 November 1984

- After being given a crash course in how to use her powers, Eleven returns from Chicago and shuts the gate to the Upside Down. Everyone is happy to see her. Well, not everyone. Creatures of the Upside Down all die – including Dustin's pet, Dart.

28 June 1985

- Russians open a small portal to the Upside Down underneath a shopping mall they built to hide their secret base of operations.

29 June 1985

- Billy Hargrove is possessed by The Mind Flayer at the Brimborn Steel Works.

2 July 1985

- Having worked out that the Russians are up to something, Steve, Robin, Erica and Dustin sneak into the Starcourt Mall loading bay and are taken in a lift to the underground heart of the military base.

3 July 1985

- Nancy and her accomplices go to the hospital to look for answers to the mysterious goings-on in Hawkins. They are attacked by a melting monster controlled by the Mind Flayer.

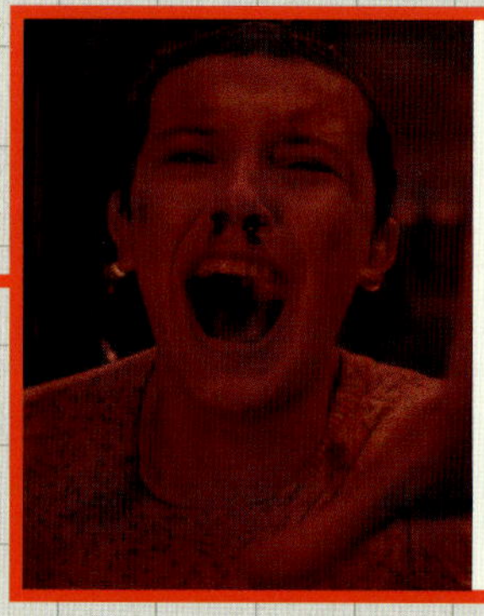

27 March 1986

- Max goes to the Creel House to lure Vecna. Eddie distracts the Demobats and dies. Max is killed and the final gate is opened. While in the Upside Down, Steve, Robin and Nancy set fire to and shoot Vecna's body to bits. Eleven brings Max back to life, but she remains in a coma.
- Hawkins is ripped apart by the enormous cracks in the earth running between Vecna's four gates from the Upside Down. Smoke curls emerge from the ground and life begins to die.

29 March 1986

- Eleven, Mike, Will and Jonathan return to Hawkins after a challenging hiatus in California and Nevada.
- Joyce, Hopper and Murray return to Hawkins after their Russian jail escapade.

10 November 1983

■ Chief Hopper discovers that the body of Will, which was found in the quarry, is a fake: a dummy filled with cotton stuffing.

11 November 1983

■ On the day of Will's funeral, Nancy Wheeler finds a portal to the Upside Down and makes a short (but not very sweet) visit.

12 November 1983

■ Joyce and Hopper enter the Upside Down through the gate at Hawkins National Laboratory and rescue Will.

13 November 1983

■ Eleven defeats the Demogorgon.

30 October 1984

■ Will Byers has a vision of the Mind Flayer, a massive, terrifying, spider-like creature.

DART

31 October 1984

■ Dustin Henderson finds a baby Demogorgon in the dustbin and adopts it.

2 November 1984

■ Investigating dying crops, Hopper digs a hole and finds a series of tunnels beneath Hawkins. He is knocked unconscious by spores.

4 July 1985

■ Steve and his associates escape the Russians.

■ The Mind Flayer crashes into the mall in a fleshy avatar comprised of the bodies of Hawkins residents.

■ Billy fights to resist the monster's possession, sacrificing himself to save Eleven. Joyce and Hopper close the gate to the Upside Down destroying the Meat Monster.

21 March 1986

■ Eddie Munson and Chrissy Cunningham are hanging out together in his Uncle's trailer when 001, now known as Vecna, kills Chrissy in a horrific and supernatural manner, in order to open the first of four gates from his world to ours.

22 March 1986

■ Vecna's second victim, Fred Benson, is taken and another gate is opened.

23 March 1986

■ After suffering from a series of symptoms, including visions, Max Mayfield reveals that she has been chosen as one of Vecna's victims, and is therefore under his curse.

24 March 1986

■ Max is captured in Vecna's Mindscape, but escapes with the help of the joyous music of Kate Bush.

25 March 1986

■ Max draws what she saw in Vecna's Mindscape and Nancy recognises it as the Creel House.

■ Lucas' teammate Patrick is Vecna's third victim.

26 March 1986

■ Nancy, Steve, Eddie, Dustin and Robin travel through the third portal, in Lover's Lake, to the Upside Down. They go to Nancy's house to get guns, but they aren't there.

U R HERE (BUT WHERE THE HELL IS THAT EXACTLY?)

Get your bearings. Can you recognise the lay of the Hawkins land and identify some of its key landmarks? You should, because you might need to run from one and hide in another.

(Clue: all the locations are dotted around this map.)

LOCATION 1.

■ Place of learning for some, place of death for the Demogorgon.

YEAR LAKE

H. HANCOCK FARM

LOCATION 3.

■ Juicy hideout for the Hawkins Tigers basketball team to cook up plans.

LOCATION 2.

■ Stop the press: this is where to find prominent members of The Flayed.

CASTLE BYERS

CREEL HOUSE

LOCATION 4.

■ Will goes there to chill and hide out – even in the Upside Down.

LOCATION 5.

■ Vecna's back-in-the-day home. The place where it all began.

NE

HAWKINS NATIONAL LABORATORY

LOCATION 7.

■ The human-puppet for the Mind Flayer made a splash here.

_ _ _ _ _ _ _

_ _ _ _ _ _ _ _ _

_ _ _ _

LOCATION 6.

■ Secret Russian base, location of 'The Key', bitchin' place to get rad new threads.

_ _ _ _ _ _ _ _ _

_ _ _ _

PALACE ARCADE

HAMPTON RD.

LOCATION 8.

■ Where the good, smoochy times at the Snow Ball were had.

_ _ _ _ _ _ _

_ _ _ _ _ _

_ _ _ _ _ _

JORDAN LAKE

HAWKINS MIDDLE SCHOOL

HERATY BRIDGE RD.

The Hawkins Post

Courage in Journalism Since 1947

LOCATION 9.

■ MADMAX was the top scorer at this high octane hangout spot.

_ _ _ _ _ _

_ _ _ _ _ _

HAWKINS COMMUNITY POOL

HAWKINS DAM

LOCATION 10.

■ In short, the scariest place to grow up/ generate electricity.

_ _ _ _ _ _ _

_ _ _ _ _ _ _ _

_ _ _ _ _ _ _ _ _ _

ANSWERS ON PAGE 118

STRANGER PEOPLE

THE CORE FOUR

'The Party' are a group of four Dungeons & Dragons enthusiasts who found themselves at the centre of a bizarre adventure that almost mirrored their board-based battles.

FOR WILL

CASE FILE: WILL

- **NAME:** Will Byers
- **NICKNAMES:** Will the Wise (good) / Zombie Boy (bad)
- **DISTINGUISHING FEATURES:** Birthmark on his right arm / hair like a hollow conker
- **SKILLS:** A talented artist / the ability to see into the Upside Down / hairs on the back of his neck stand up
- **TRAITS:** Reserved / strong / supportive / tetchy / jealous

WILL THE WISE

CLERIC

LIKES.
NINTENDO, REESE'S PIECES, THE X-MEN, THE CLASH.

DISLIKES.
BEING THE THIRD WHEEL, GROWING UP.

Will: The ultimate survivor

"WHEN YOU'RE DIFFERENT, SOMETIMES YOU FEEL LIKE A MISTAKE."

Mike: Team leader Wheeler

CASE FILE: MIKE

- **NAME:** Mike Wheeler
- **NICKNAME:** Frog-face (bad)
- **DISTINGUISHING FEATURES:** Twig-like body / pouty with a heavy fringe
- **TALENTS:** Effective leader / strategist / excellent Dungeon Master
- **TRAITS:** Loyal / moody / protective

"I'M NOT EXACTLY MR POPULARITY."

CASE FILE: DUSTIN

- **NAME:** Dustin Henderson
- **NICKNAMES:** Dusty (mum) / Dusty-bun (Suzie)
- **PETS:** Mews the orange cat / Tews the Siamese cat / Yurtle the tortoise / Dart the Demodog
- **SKILLS:** Excellent English accent / terrific singing voice
- **TRAITS:** Calm /clever / always carries batteries
- **FAVE ARCADE GAMES:** Dragon's Lair and Dig Dug

Dustin: Doofus with brains

"I WAS THE ONLY REASONABLE ONE."

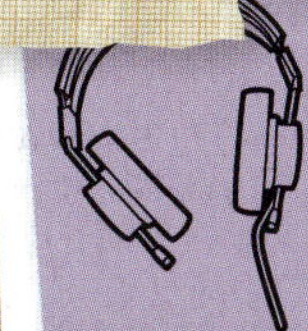

FUN FACT.

DUSTIN MOVED TO HAWKINS IN THE FOURTH GRADE.

CAMP KNOW WHERE

Lucas: Cautious but kind

CASE FILE: LUCAS

- **NAME:** Lucas Sinclair
- **NICKNAMES:** Stalker (coined by Max)
- **DISTINGUISHING FEATURES:** Camouflage bandana / utility belt / catapault
- **SKILLS:** Excellent aim with a slingshot
- **TRAITS:** Impulsive / headstrong / suspicious / prepared
- **WEAKNESS:** Jealous of being replaced by Eleven

"I'M TIRED OF BEING BULLIED."

MAX

RANGER

Lucas Sinclair

LIKES.

NEW COKE, FIREWORKS, MAX'S LAUGH.

DISLIKES.

3 MUSKETEERS CHOCOLATE.

LIKES.

WALKIE TALKIES, STAR WARS, WILL'S DRAWINGS, PICKING FLOWERS FOR EL.

DISLIKES.

HIGH SCHOOL, HIS MUM HOGGING THE PHONE, SAYING THE WORD 'LOVE'.

THE BIG KIDS

Babysitters of Hawkins arm yourselves and unite and kiss, or don't kiss, it's totally your call.

Nancy: Small but deadly

LIKES.
JOURNALING AND BLONDIE.

DISLIKES.
TAKING NO FOR AN ANSWER.

FIRST GIRL

Nancy is the first person to go into the Upside Down and return to tell the tale.

"ASK FORGIVENESS, NOT PERMISSION."

CASE FILE: NANCY

- **NAME:** Nancy Wheeler
- **NICKNAMES:** Little Miss Perfect / The Princess / Nancy Drew
- **DISTINGUISHING FEATURES:** Frilly blouses / big hair / a sawn-off shotgun
- **TALENT:** Excellent shot / detective
- **TRAITS:** Fearless / caring / natural leader / thoughtful / smart
- **BAD HABITS:** Breaking hearts / accidentally leading friends to their doom

Don't panic, maybe love will save us!

CASE FILE: JONATHAN

- **NAME:** Jonathan Byers
- **NICKNAMES:** Mopey Dick (attrib: Argyle)
- **DISTINGUISHING FEATURES:** Shaggy hair /carrying a camera
- **TALENT:** Excellent shot / detective
- **SKILLS:** Making mixtapes / making spiky weapons / pep talks / giving hugs / setting fire to Demogorgons
- **TRAITS:** Loving / weird / awkward / pessimistic / quiet / hopeful

Jonathan: In a mood since 1982

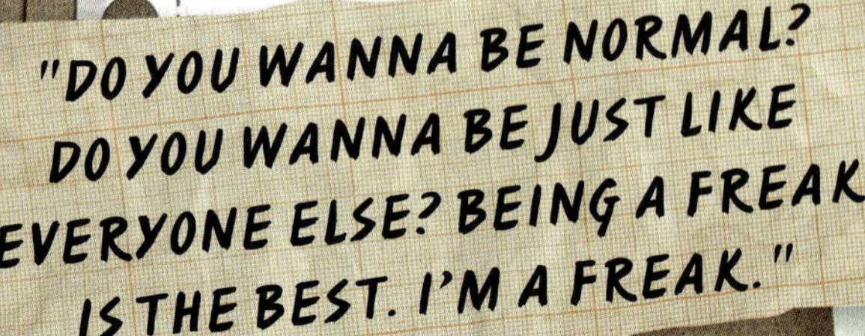

LIKES.
THE CLASH, KURT VONNEGUT, THE EVIL DEAD, TALKING HEADS.

DISLIKES.
HUNTING, GOING TO PARTIES.

CASE FILE: STEVE

- **NAME:** Steve Harrington
- **NICKNAMES:** King Steve / Steve 'the hair' Harrington
- **DISTINGUISHING FEATURES:** Thick luxurious hair
- **TRAITS:** Overly protective / brave / thoughtful / helpful
- **WEAKNESS:** Flirting / forgetting to bring a torch
- **WANTS:** 6 children: 3 boys, 3 girls
- **BAD HABITS:** Smashing cameras / knowing virtually nothing about anything / peeing wherever he likes – elevators, you name it ...

Steve: The hair maketh the man

The cool guy and the Queen of Scoops

"I'M A PRETTY DAMN GOOD BABYSITTER."

LIKES.
KFC, FARRAH FAWCETT HAIRSPRAY.

DISLIKES.
BABYSITTING (OR DOES HE?).

PLACE OF WORK
SCOOPS AHOY, FAMILY VIDEO

"the hair"

CASE FILE: ROBIN

- **NAME:** Robin Buckley
- **DISTINGUISHING FEATURES:** Messy brown bob / sassy-tongued gob
- **TRAITS:** Ditzy / awkward / chatty / funny / honest / anxious
- **TALENT:** Excellent shot / detective
- **SKILLS:** Learning Russian / playing the trumpet / talking her way into mental asylums
- **WEAKNESS:** Walking in heels / running weirdly

Robin: Code-breaker, itchy blouse-hater

"I CAN'T BELIEVE I'M GOING TO DIE IN A SECRET RUSSIAN BASE WITH STEVE 'THE HAIR' HARRINGTON."

CRUSHES

Tammy Thompson and Vickie, the Molly Ringwald look-alike from band.

STRANGER PEOPLE

ELEVEN

Some superheroes are born great and other have greatness thrust upon them. For Eleven, the lab-raised saviour of Hawkins, both are scarily true.

■ Even superheroes need tissues

■ Jane Hopper is plaid to the bone

■ Life isn't all rosy for Eleven

■ When 'show and tell' is utter hell

■ Eleven is 'armed' and dangerous

CASE FILE: ELEVEN

- **NAME:** 011, Eleven
- **NICKNAMES:** Jane Ives, El, Brat (by Hopper, on a bad day)
- **DISTINGUISHING FEATURES:** Buzzcut / curly hair / blonde wig / outstretched arm / bloody nose
- **SKILLS:** Moving objects and matter with her mind / ripping holes in the fabric of space and time / finding and spying on people
- **WEAKNESS:** Using her powers for too long knocks her out

Cabin fever is about to kick in

HIDEOUT:
HOPPER'S GRANDFATHER'S CABIN

LIKES: TRIPLE-DECKER EGGO EXTRAVAGANZAS, WATCHING WESTERNS WITH HOPPER, PINEAPPLE ON PIZZA.

D&D ROLE: MAGE

THE 'NOT STUPID' CABIN RULES:

RULE NUMBER 1.
KEEP THE CURTAINS CLOSED.

RULE NUMBER 2.
ONLY OPEN THE DOOR TO HOPPER'S SECRET KNOCK.

RULE NUMBER 3.
NEVER GO OUT ALONE, ESPECIALLY IN THE DAYLIGHT.

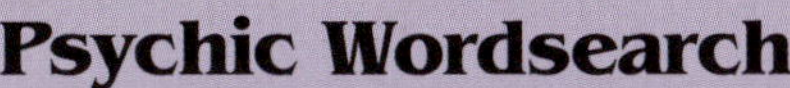

Out of context quote:

"I PIGGYBACKED FROM A PIZZA DOUGH FREEZER."

El enters The Void

Psychic Wordsearch

Can you find all the words that Eleven was made to guess during an experiment she took part in at Hawkins Lab?

Begin / Amulet / Frigid / Evolve / Airplane / Eleven / Peninsula / Game / Mouse / Balloon

E	N	O	O	L	L	A	B	J	P
I	N	A	M	U	L	E	T	E	J
T	C	A	P	L	F	O	N	V	W
D	R	P	L	R	K	I	Q	M	D
N	W	B	I	P	N	T	O	B	S
C	E	G	C	S	R	U	A	E	H
W	I	V	U	Q	S	I	Z	G	D
D	B	L	E	E	O	V	A	I	P
Y	A	Z	P	L	Z	W	P	N	M
E	V	L	O	V	E	E	M	A	G

Being on the run = fast food

ANSWERS ON PAGE 118

ELECTRONICS

OMG Gnarly!

11 TIMES ELEVEN ATE

No matter how many times you see Eleven use her telekinetic powers it's always astonishing. These psychic showdowns are next-level incredible.

11. Can she crush it?

■ El's act of **crushing a Coke can with her mind** is simple enough, but it still leaves you breathless the first time you see it.

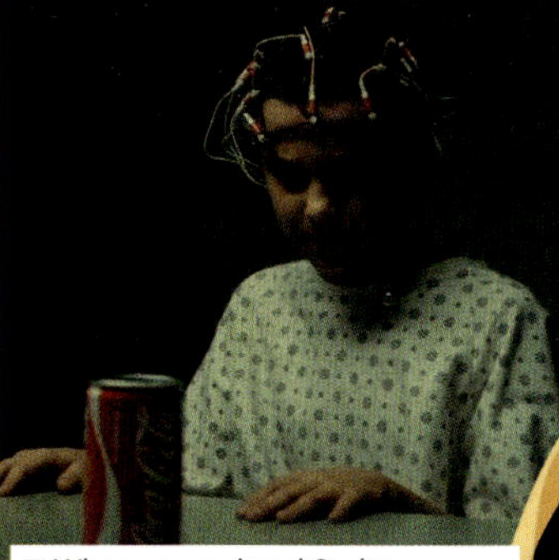

■ When you ordered Sprite ...

10. Fan service

■ White noise is the worst. Eleven **stops an annoyingly noisy fan** at Benny's Burgers from ... well, being annoying.

■ The OG in noise-cancelling tech

■ It's not stealing, it's borrowing forever

9. Waffley petty

■ When Eleven **stole a bunch of Eggo frozen waffles from the local store**, she did not have to smash the shop windows when she left, but when a person is at the absolute end of their tether, you have to expect that level of pettiness.

8. Shoplifting (for real this time)

■ When a shopkeeper turned a gun on her buddy Kali, Eleven did what she does best and **tossed him across the room like** he was nothing but a grubby hoody.

■ Do not mock El's hair gel - EVER

■ Hey Mike, need a lift?

7. Mike flies

■ School bully Troy threatened to hurt Dustin unless Mike jumped into the quarry. He did it, but before he hit the water El turned up, **stopped him in mid-air and floated him back to solid ground**. Then she broke Troy's arm. Ouch.

6. Full throttle

■ Eleven took a step into the dark side when she used her powers to **strangle one of "the bad men" that tortured her mother.** Thankfully, she stopped herself before going too far, remembering that *she* wasn't the monster – they were.

■ One look was all it took

5. Chopper horror

■ If you send someone in pursuit of Eleven, you'd better prepare for the worst. How do people not know this? Of course, the helicopter chasing her is going to **fall from the sky and explode into a fiery ball**. What did they expect?

■ Not gonna fly with Jane Ives

4. Flippin' eck

■ The first time "the bad men" in white vans pursue El and the gang, it looks like there's no escape. How can bikes outrun a persistent fleet of vehicles? Well, Eleven psychically plucked one off the road, **tossed it into the air like it was a peanut**, and that, was pretty much the end of that.

■ Bad men van-quished

■ Not the time for rock, paper, scissors

3. Demogorgon death

■ El **pins a Demogorgon against the wall and explodes it into smithereens.** Equal parts terrifying and stupefying.

2. Slamming the gate shut

■ Eleven's greatest challenge came when she had to **close the gate between worlds**. That took a lot of concentration, a lot of power and rather a lot of bloody snot.

■ Closing time for the Upside Down

■ 011 turns 001's world upside down

1. Outta this world punishment

■ Not a permanent solution and not one without serious repercussions, but when Eleven **banished the murderously evil Henry Creel into another dimension**, it was her single greatest act. Bye-bye psycho.

LET'S NOT FORGET

Pee pants Troy

Eleven proved that she's the superhero we all need by making bully Troy pee his pants, in front of the whole school.

Chocs Away

How would most of us use powers, if we had them? Emptying all the chocolate from a vending machine? El did this at the hospital in 1985.

STRANGER PEOPLE

SIDE-KICK CITY

The best friends you could ever hope to have, laugh with, fall in love with ... and a couple of absolutely bad and cracked eggs.

CASE FILE: MAX

"GAG ME WITH A SPOON."

- **NAME:** Max Mayfield
- **NICKNAMES:** Mad Max / Red
- **DISTINGUISHING FEATURES:** Red hair / Walkman / skateboard / eyes that roll back into her head
- **SKILLS:** Skateboarding / letter writing / putting together looks (at the mall)
- **TRAITS:** Strong-willed / guarded / sarcastic / feminist who doesn't let boys get away with bad behaviour

Max: Just call her Skate Bush

LIKES.
'RUNNING UP THAT HILL' BY KATE BUSH, TEEN MAGAZINES, DIGDUG.

DISLIKES.
BEING SPIED ON BY CREEPS, FEELING GUILTY FOR BILLY'S DEATH.

CASE FILE: ERICA

- **NAME:** Erica Sinclair
- **NICKNAME:** Lady Applejack
- **DISTINGUISHING FEATURES:** Sunny bright wardrobe of pink turquoise and yellow that does not match her sassy mouth
- **SKILLS:** Handy with a cattle prod / negotiating / crawling through small spaces / knowing her worth and fighting for what she deserves
- **D&D ROLE:** Chaotic-good, half-elf rogue, level 14

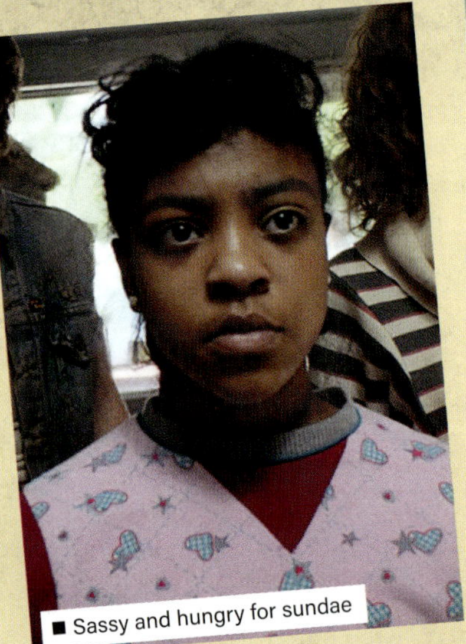

Sassy and hungry for sundae

LIKES.
ICE CREAM WITH HOT FUDGE SAUCE.

DISLIKES.
BORING BOXES AND NERDS (BUT NOT REALLY).

"PLEASE DON'T CRY NERDS."

"HOLD ONTO YOUR BUTTS, BROCHACHOS!"

CASE FILE: ARGYLE

- **JOB:** Surfer Boy Pizza
- **DESCRIBED AS:** A little on the eccentric side / funny
- **DISTINGUISHING FEATURES:** Yellow Surfer Boy Pizza visor and T-shirt / Hawaiian shirts / waist-length poker-straight hair
- **SKILLS:** Chilling everyone out / foraging for mushrooms
- **LIKES:** Pineapple on a pizza, schmacking good risotto
- **DISLIKES:** Bad government dudes with guns

CASE FILE: SUZIE

"PLANCK'S CONSTANT IS 6.62607004."

- **NAME:** Suzie Bingham
- **NICKNAMES:** Suzie Poo
- **DISTINGUISHING FEATURES:** Glasses / sweater vests
- **SKILLS:** Computer hacking / geolocation / mathematical equations
- **TRAITS:** Firm and fair / romantic / rule-abiding / intelligent
- **LIKES:** The Wizard of Oz / The Wizard of Earthsea / Jesus
- **DISLIKES:** Swearing / being taken for granted

"MY BRAIN'S JUST BEEN A LITTLE FRAZZLED LATELY."

CASE FILE: VICKIE

- **DISTINGUISHING FEATURES:** short red hair / rosy cheeks
- **TRAITS:** Sweet rambling chatterbox
- **SKILLS:** Making peanut butter-on-peanut butter monstrosities for the needy
- **LIKES:** Fast Times at Ridgemont High / playing in band
- **DISLIKES:** Her ex-boyfriend / Tammie Thompson's Muppet voice
- **WEAKNESS:** Phoebe Cates (allegedly – according to Steve)

CASE FILE: KALI

"I CAN MAKE PEOPLE SEE OR NOT SEE WHATEVER I CHOOSE."

- **NICKNAME:** 008
- **ESCAPED FROM HAWKINS LAB:** Sometime before 1979
- **DISTINGUISHING FEATURES:** punky purple side-sweep undercut
- **SKILLS:** Giving people visions of whatever she chooses
- **TRAITS:** Ruthless / lonely / lost
- **LIKES:** Reconnecting with her 'sister' Jane Ives aka 011
- **DISLIKES:** Dr Brenner / just about everyone else

STRANGER PEOPLE

YOU SUCK / YOU RULE

Not every adult is a double-crossing Lando*. You can trust some of them. Memorise this handy cheat sheet.

YOU SUCK

I LIKE IT COLD

DR MARTIN BRENNER

'Papa,' is anything but a father figure. Loving, caring and supportive? – not much. Cruel, conniving, manipulative and sadistic? – most def.

AGENT CONNIE FRAZIER

A nasty piece of work who shot and killed Benny, who was only trying to be a good citizen. Eleven un-alived her before decimating the Demogorgon.

MAYOR LARRY KLINE

Corrupt politician? Who ever heard of such a thing? Disgraced former Mayor Klein was arrested for doing secret deals with the Russians – namely allowing them to open a portal to the Upside Down. Anything for a couple of bucks, eh?

LT COLONEL JACK SULLIVAN

Dude is unforgiving and ruthless. Do not approach, under any circumstances. He will not listen to your spluttering explanations. National security is his hobby and your feeble life is getting in its way.

LONNIE BYERS

Will's dad is a deadbeat waste of space. Not only did he make Jonathan kill a rabbit on his 10th birthday, but when he thought Will was dead, the scuzzbag came searching for financial compensation.

TOM HOLLOWAY

Nancy and Jonathan's boss at The Hawkins Post was a sexist pig. He totally deserved to be melted down as part of the 'Hospital monster.'

GRIGORI

The terrifying Russian hitman who killed Alexei at the funfair. Not cool. Very uncool actually.

* Nerd alert! Lando Calrissian is a character in Star Wars: Empire Strikes Back, who double-crosses his old friend, Han Solo.

YOU RULE

NO.1 FAN

CHIEF JIM HOPPER

Sloppy but brilliant Police Chief who believes that: "Mornings are for coffee and contemplation." He is the best of us. We don't deserve him, etc, etc ...

DR SAM OWENS

Dr Sam Owens is a senior figure working at Hawkins National Lab, but unlike his colleague, Dr Brenner, he isn't a steaming pile of dog sick. It was Dr Owens who helped Hopper adopt Eleven, and when El lost her powers he did everything he could to help her get them back.

MR CLARKE

If only all science teachers were this great. Scott Clarke always makes time for his students, even when they interrupt his weekend VCR movie night to enquire about floatation tanks. Far be it for him to keep curiosity doors locked.

MURRAY BAUMAN

"My fingers are like arrows! My arms, like iron! My feet, like spears! Resist, and I will end you!" is something that Murray once boasted. Was he lying? Does it matter? In reality the investigative journalist and karate fan is eccentric but smart with a good-heart.

JOYCE BYERS

The desperate mother who will do anything for her kids, but insists: "I'm not crazy!" She isn't crazy, she just really loves Christmas decorations.

DR ALEXEI

After switching sides, Alexei was having the time of his life, experiencing cherry Slushies and giant fluffy funfair prizes. But defecting and double-crossing has repercussions, like Arnie-wannabes playing out their 'Hasta La Vista' fantasies.

DIMITRI ANTONOV

Russian prison guards are human after all, well at least this one. Dimitri played against type and helped Hopper escape from a maximum-security Demogorgon-death gulag. The definition of a true comrade.

KAREN WHEELER

The mother of Mike and Nancy has had it, especially with her husband, who enjoys a good meal and not much else. "I hope you're enjoying your chicken, Ted." A fan of romance novels and catching rays (and feelings) at the community swimming pool.

BOB NEWBY

Some believed Joyce and Hopper were destined to be together, but for a while Bob was the owner of the wholesome shoulder Joyce Byers took comfort on. That is until a pack of Demodogs ate Bob. Sob!

STRANGER PEOPLE

GONE, GONE, GONE!

Let's remember the Hawkins residents who left their mark on the town and then left the town – because they died and went to heaven – or hell – both are popular options.

CASE FILE: EDDIE

- **NAME:** Eddie Munson
- **NICKNAMES:** Eddie the Banished / The Freak
- **DISTINGUISHING FEATURES:** Doe eyes (according to Robin) / long wavy hair / Hellfire T-shirt / indeterminate age
- **SKILLS:** Hot-wiring a car / shredding the electric guitar
- **TRAITS:** Outgoing / funny / forgiving / loud / scared / heroic
- **D&D ROLE:** Dungeon Master

"IT'S FORCED CONFORMING. THAT'S WHAT'S KILLING THE KIDS. THAT'S THE REAL MONSTER."

Metal as a toaster!

LIKES. IRON MAIDEN AND METALLICA.

DISLIKES. DEMOBATS AND BASKETBALL.

DIED 4 JULY 1985

CASE FILE: BILLY

- **NAME:** Billy Hargrove
- **NICKNAME:** Keg King
- **DISTINGUISHING FEATURES:** Tight jeans / straggly, blond mullet / when Flayed – massively sweaty
- **SKILLS:** Strength / surfing
- **DESCRIBED AS:** "Angry all the time" and "Really gross" (attrib: Max)
- **TRAITS:** Mean / vain / insecure / unhappy / angry
- **HOBBIES:** Working out / being adored / bullying people

Not bad, just messed up

LIKES. HEAVY METAL, CARS AND DOUBLE DENIM.

DISLIKES. BUTTONS ON SHIRTS AND HAWKINS.

"NO ONE TELLS ME WHAT TO DO."

BILLY HARGROVE
MAR. 29 1967
JUL. 4 1985
GONE BUT NOT FORGOTTEN

DIED 8 NOV 1983

"I'M CHILL."

CASE FILE: BARB

- **NAME:** Barbra Holland
- **FUN FACT:** Robin was Barb's childhood best friend
- **DISTINGUISHING FEATURES:** Massive glasses / frilly tops / short, wavy, dark red curls
- **SKILLS:** Observation – she notices Nancy is wearing a new bra
- **LAST SEEN:** On Steve Harrington's diving board
- **LIKES:** Frilly pie-crust necklines / gently mocking Nancy
- **DISLIKES:** People not being true to themselves / bullies

"DO YOU EVER FEEL LIKE YOU'RE LOSING YOUR MIND?"

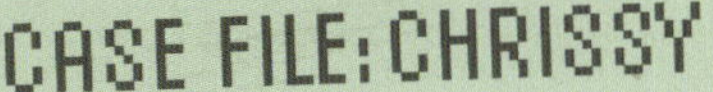

CASE FILE: CHRISSY

- **NAME:** Chrissy Cunningham
- **NICKNAMES:** The Queen of Hawkins High
- **DISTINGUISHING FEATURES:** Strawberry blonde hair / signature ponytail / green scrunchie / blue eyeshadow / Cheer Squad uniform
- **SKILLS:** Cheerleading
- **TRAITS:** Polite / sweet / shy
- **LIKES:** Eddie Munson – which came as something of a surprise
- **DISLIKES:** Her mother commenting on her appearance

DIED 21 MARCH 1986

DIED 27 MARCH 1986

GO TIGERS!

CASE FILE: JASON

- **NAME:** Jason Carver
- **CAPTAIN:** Hawkins High basketball team, the Hawkins Tigers
- **DISTINGUISHING FEATURES:** Green letterman jacket / blond hair / scowl
- **SKILLS:** Dribbling / punching
- **TRAITS:** Loyal / angry / sad / mean / self-righteous
- **LIKES:** Winning / giving long boring speeches / ThunderCats
- **DISLIKES:** The Hellfire 'devil worshipping' cult

DON'T FORGET FRED AND PATRICK. (VECNA WOULD NEVER)

"HOW DO YOU EXPECT TO STOP THE DEVIL IF YOU DON'T BELIEVE HE'S REAL?"

TEST SUBJECT

GUESS WHO IN HAWKINS!

Can you spot a friend or foe at fifty paces – in the dark, upside down in a void?

SUBJECT NOTES

Good girl gone mad

NAME

1 _ _ _ _ _

SUBJECT NOTES

Oh baby (sitter)

NAME

2 _ _ _ _ _ _

SUBJECT NOTES

Alright petal

NAME

3 _ _ _ _ _ _ _ _ _ _

SUBJECT NOTES

Lawful good

NAME

4 _ _ _ _ _ _

SUBJECT NOTES

Not the right way up

NAME

5 _ _ _ _ _

SUBJECT NOTES

Nerds beware

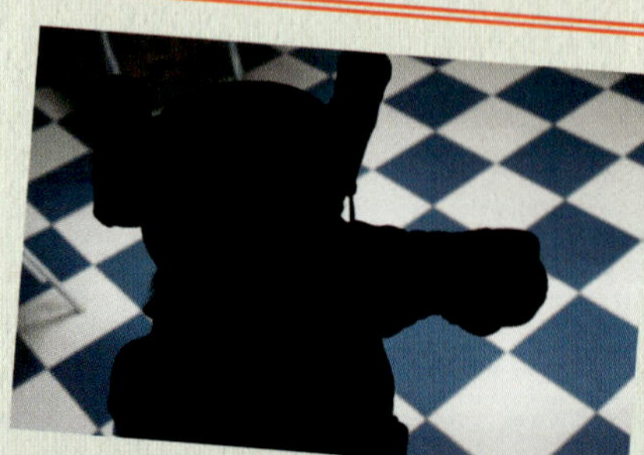

NAME

6 _ _ _ _ _

SUBJECT NOTES

Get her number

NAME

7 _ _ _ _ _ _

SUBJECT NOTES

Get it hot like Papa

NAME

8 _ _/_ _ _ _ _ _ _ _

SUBJECT NOTES

Tiger in training

NAME

9 _ _ _ _ _ _

SUBJECT NOTES

Paper-thin victim

NAME

10 _ _ _ _

SUBJECT NOTES

Not very orderly

NAME

11 _ _ _ _ _ _

HAWKINS NATIONAL LABORATORY
U.S. DEPT OF ENERGY

THE UPSIDE

Answers on page 118

WELCOME TO HAWKINS

STRANGER PLACES

11 HAWKINS HOTSPOTS TO DIE FOR

There's loads to see in Hawkins, sadly most of it will get you killed. Here's a handy guide of where to go and where to maybe avoid.

■ A great place to dump an old Fiat or hide

SAFE-ISH

HAWKINS JUNKYARD

TRAILER PARK

■ A wheely good home from home

DANGEROUS

■ Place of natural beauty – just don't fall in!

SAFE-ISH

SATTLER QUARRY

BRIMBORN STEEL WORKS

■ Don't be a melt, and avoid the town's unofficial metal asylum

VERY DANGEROUS

■ Has the best science teacher ever!

HAWKINS MIDDLE SCHOOL

SAFE-ISH

ROANE HILL CEMETARY

■ Going here could be a grave mistake

■ Quite chill, as long as you're on the right side of the bars

PENHURST MENTAL HOSPITAL

■ The lifeguard might not fulfil the duties of his job description

HAWKINS COMMUNITY POOL

■ Captalism is flawed, but communism is also a worry

STARCOURT MALL

■ Avoid Keith and you'll be fine

PALACE ARCADE

■ Their experiments are on people and demon dimensions. Go absolutely anywhere else. Even the dentist

HAWKINS NATIONAL LABORATORY

STRANGER PLACES

STARCOURT MALL

The most exciting place in Hawkins to spend your allowance.

■ The shiny, all-new **Starcourt Mall** arrived in Hawkins in 1985. It seemed to spring up from nowhere, but no one cared about that. It was a modern state-of-the-art lifestyle experience, bringing the best of the 80s to an Indiana backwater. But, it wasn't cheap, a drawback for those shopping for affordable gifts.

LYNX TRANSPORTATION CORP IS NOT A TAXI SERVICE. STOP HAILING OUR SECRET TRUCKS!

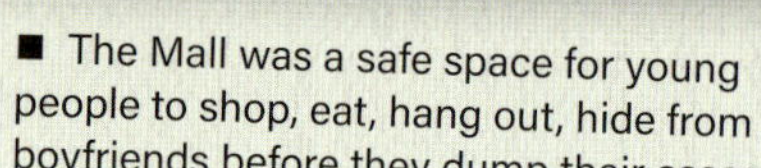

■ The Mall was a safe space for young people to shop, eat, hang out, hide from boyfriends before they dump their asses.

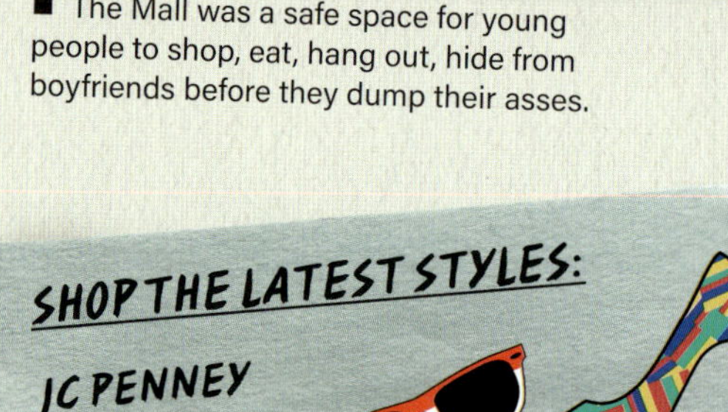

SHOP THE LATEST STYLES:

JC PENNEY
GADZOOKS
THE GAP
FASHION BUG
SEARS
CASUAL CORNER
LANE BRYANT
CLAIRE'S

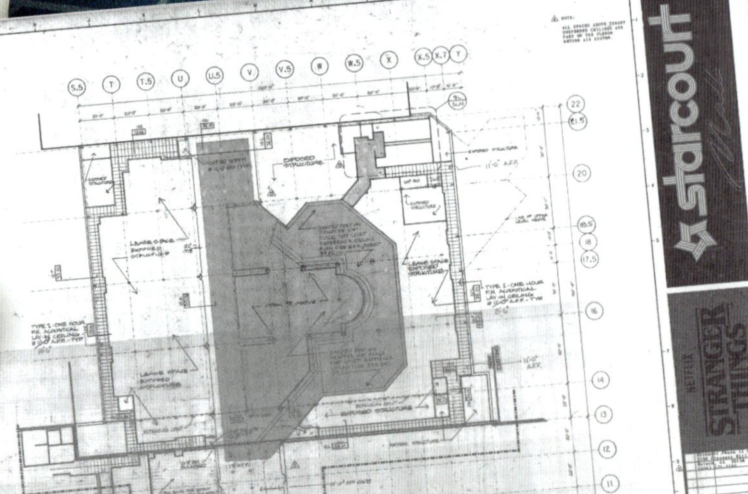

Scoops Troop
Unlimited ice cream samples at **Scoops Ahoy** while stocks last. Try **U.S.S. Butterscotch**, it's an unsinkable taste sensation.
GOOD EATING AT THE FOOD COURT:
SCOOPS AHOY
HOT SAM PRETZELS
NEW YORK PIZZA
TACO BELL
ORANGE JULIUS
GREAT PANDA
THE COOKIE COMPANY
starcourt
STRANGER THINGS
RTKL
The FOOD COURT
YAY! CAPITALISM! SO GOOD, NOT LIKE STINKY COMMUNISM – BLEUCH!
MELVALD'S GENERAL STORE IS RUBBISH. DON'T GO THERE, COMRADE.
MAYOR LARRY KLINE SAYS:
DON'T DRINK THE TOXIC CHEMICALS
10% OFF FERTILISER FOR THE FLAYED
IGNORE THE MEAN-LOOKING RUSSIANS
NO INTERDIMENSIONAL RUPTURE TO SEE HERE
starcourt Mall
starcourt

HAWKINS NATIONAL LABORATORY
U.S. DEPT OF ENERGY

STRANGER PLACES

HAWKINS NATIONAL LABORATORY

The Hawkins Lab pretended to be the Department of Energy, but it was a lot more than that. It was a secret research facility for gifted children. Children that the government wished to turn into weapons!

■ For a supposed power and light company, Hawkins Lab was pretty dark.

■ Hawkins National Laboratory was run by Director of Operations, **Dr Martin Brenner**, who the child subjects called 'Papa.' Papa was no cuddly father figure, he was a tough-as-nails disciplinarian who almost seemed to enjoy pushing the children to the point of pain with electric-shock collars.

hnl
HAWKINS NATIONAL LABORATORY
U.S. DEPT OF ENERGY
ALL ACCESS
6998-1679
DR. MARTIN BRENNER
DIRECTOR

■ **The Rainbow Room** was the best room in the Lab. The place where the children got to play and test their capabilities with a series of 'fun' games.

■ The child subjects regularly **participated in experiments** that explored their psychic abilities.

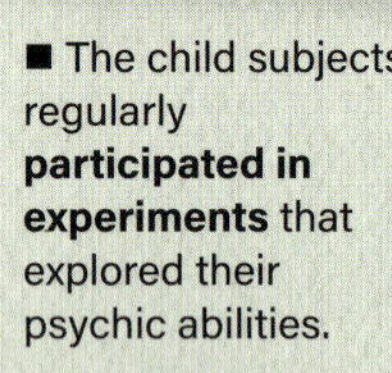

■ Each child had their **own numbered room**, but it was nothing like a hotel – no cable TV, no fluffy towels, no tea and biscuits.

■ Despite not showing much initial skill, **Eleven was Dr Brenner's favourite 'pupil'.** He believed in her, somehow sensing an untapped potential.

■ **The flotation tank** enabled Eleven to travel remotely through The Void to watch and listen to people elsewhere in the world.

■ **Henry appeared to be a laboratory orderly**, there to help the 'subjects' trapped in the windowless fortress. In actual fact he was Vecna-in-waiting.

■ Henry actively tried to get Eleven on 'his side' by revealing little bits of information about the history of Hawkins Lab. He confided in Eleven, gaining her trust by **revealing his tattoo** and letting her know that – shhhh – he was subject 001.

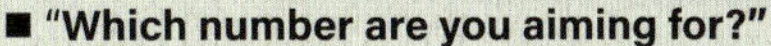

■ **"Which number are you aiming for?"**
Henry developed a bond with Eleven, simply by taking an interest in her. He gave her advice on how best to harness her powers. He told her the truth about her mother. However, he did not tell her the truth about being a psychopathic killer.

■ Henry showed Eleven a way out of Hawkins Lab: **a secret tunnel** that she could escape through. A good thing.

■ **Henry lied to Eleven,** telling her that the other children were planning to kill her, and that Dr Brenner wants that to happen. A bad thing. Soon after this, Eleven removed the 'Soteria' chip in Henry's neck, that suppressed his powers – which lead to the 1979 massacre. After which, HNL would never be the same.

LEAVING
HAWKINS
COME AGAIN SOON

STRANGER PLACES

BEYOND HAWKINS

The story of Hawkins actually stretches far and wide, even wider than the infamous tunnel system.

CALIFORNIA

In 1985, Eleven and the Byers clan **relocated to Lenora Hills**, a small community in California to get away from it all and put their pasts (and the chaotic mess of Hawkins) behind them. It was supposed to be a quiet and nice new life, but **bullies are everywhere** and they can make your life miserable even without the powers of an evil entity. On the upside Jonathan made a new friend, Argyle, a **cool dude** with easy access to pizza.

Surfer Boy Pizza

PINK O-MANIA

CHICAGO

After years of being locked up, going to her first **big city** was an eye-opener for Eleven. The people were a bit scary, but at least they had Eggos: which she **stole by the armful**. Someone really needs to give this girl some pocket money. El stayed in the city long enough to learn a few **important life-lessons**: what to do, and what not to do.

NEVADA

Just because Hawkins National Lab was shut down, doesn't mean that the **experimental work** stopped. It just upped sticks and moved to the desert, where there were fewer prying eyes, and less likelihood of a breach from beneath them. **The Nina Project** was set up to try and restore El's powers. To achieve this, Dr Brenner and Dr Owens repurposed a space that had previously been a **missile silo**.

Dr Owens met Eleven to talk her into participating in his 'Nina' project. They presumably met on the State border of Nevada and California.

SALT LAKE CITY

Suzie lives on the other side of the country in Utah. It's a 23 hour drive away, so it's no wonder that Dustin and his girlfriend, who is **definitely real**, keep in touch via **radio transmissions**. Half of the gang finally paid Suzie a visit in 1986 to help them track down Eleven.

RUSSIA

When the Russians discovered that the Americans had a **gateway to another world** they wanted to know more. They created their own experimental project **Starcourt Base** under The Starcourt Mall. When that rigmarole came to light and was shut down, they regrouped back in the motherland, taking some creatures from the Upside Down, and Jim Hopper with them. Hopper was **thrown into prison** in Siberia, and if it hadn't been for the kind intervention of Soviet guard Dimitri Antonov, he might never have escaped, or worse, been fed to a **captive Demogorgon**. In order to rescue Hopper, Joyce and Murray paid a visit to Yuri's Fish N' Fly – a **totally legit business** and not a **smuggling operation** at all.

HAWKINS NATIONAL LABORATORY
U.S. DEPT OF ENERGY

OMG Gnarly!

SHOWDOWN AT HAWKINS LAB

Before Vecna, the number one scariest thing in Eleven's life was the friendly orderly who went full throttle mental.

AND THEN THERE WAS ONE

Date: 8th September 1979.

Location: Hawkins National Laboratory

Event: Henry Creel, aka test-subject 001, goes on a murderous rampage through the Hawkins Lab killing everyone he can ... until he's finally stopped by a 'friend'!

■ The events of 1979 were so shocking and upsetting that Eleven's brain had done its best to forget all about it. But parts of the horrible day repeatedly flashed in her mind. **When she remembered being covered in blood**, Eleven assumed that she'd lost her temper and it was she who had killed everyone in the HNL psychic-program.

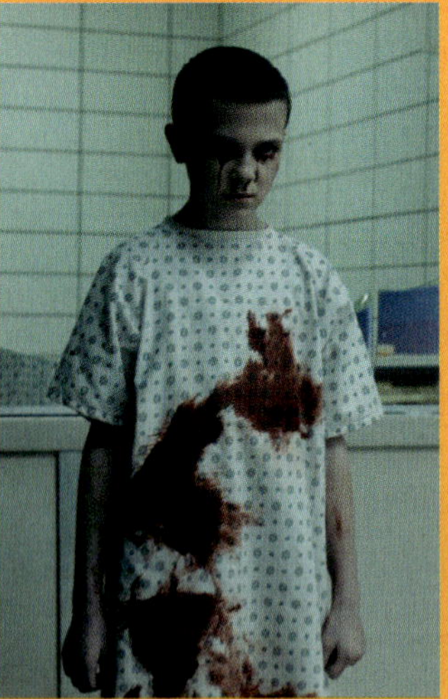

■ Like all of the children, Eleven had assumed that **Henry was a harmless orderly employed to help out at Hawkins Lab**. She had no idea that he was the first test-subject, that he had unmatched psychic powers, or that he'd use them in such a vicious way.

"We're alike. You and I."

001 to 011

■ Henry had formed a bond with Eleven. He saw himself in her and he wanted to let her live. But **Eleven was so horrified by what he'd done** that of course she couldn't 'join him', she had to stop him!

■ Henry started out strong, **lifting Eleven off the floor, twisting her poor body**, but incredibly, she resisted, breaking out of his psychic grip.

"It's time you were free from this hell."

Henry

■ **Eleven fought and defeated Henry** by using his own advice against him. When Henry told Eleven to harness emotional memories to fuel her psychic attacks, he didn't realise that he was sealing his own fate – banishment to an un-earthly nether realm.

■ **Eleven threw Henry through a window** and pinned him against the wall. A move she would later use on the Demogorgon. She then blew him into a gazillion pieces. The psychic energy was so powerful that it created a rift in space-time pushing what remained of Henry into another dimension.

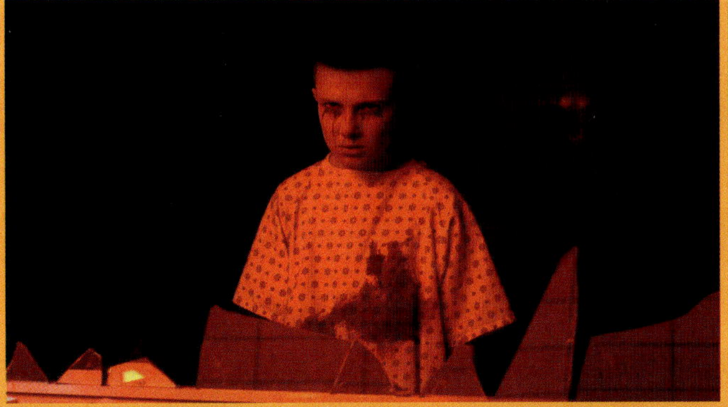

■ Eleven had thought that she was the reason everyone died that day, but the blood splattered all over her was her own. She alone had stopped the evil madman. She was the hero, not the monster. Why had no one ever told her?

■ With all the other subjects now gone, Dr Brenner concentrated all of his efforts on his last remaining test subject: 011.

HOW TO:

With a pen or pencil trace your way around the Lab, avoiding the monsters and dead ends. The right path will take you past each Party member as you go. Leave no one behind.

TEST SUBJECT

ESCAPE FROM HAWKINS LAB

El has lost her powers. You're the only one who can save Hawkins. Are you in (and then hopefully out)?

CODE RED

This is not a drill. Your mission – enter Hawkins National Laboratory, sneak past the Demodogs, Demogorgon and Vecna, steal Dr Brenner's Access All Areas pass, initiate the self-destruct protocols, blow the place to smithereens and RUNNNN! Oh, and you have to rescue Will, Lucas, Dustin and Mike along the way. Sound doable? It's actually almost impossible, but in the words of Dusty Bun (via Han Solo): "never tell me the odds." Oh, too late. Sorry. Go, go, GO!!!

hnl
HAWKINS NATIONAL LABORATORY
U.S. DEPT OF ENERGY
ALL ACCESS
DR. MARTIN BRENNER
DIRECTOR

SELF DESTRUCT
...YOU HAVE 10 SECONDS TO EVACUATE

EXIT

ANSWERS ON PAGE 118

GAME OVER

STRANGER WORLDS

THE UPSIDE DOWN

Imagine a scarier version of your town, filled with terrifying creatures. Well, the people of Hawkins don't have to imagine ...

WHAT IS THE UPSIDE DOWN?

The Upside Down is ... upside down, until you fall through a gate into it and then you're the right way up again. The physics is bonkers, but then so are vicious flower-faced entities.

Dustin compared the Upside Down to a spooky world from Dungeons & Dragons:

"The Vale of Shadows is a dimension that is a dark reflection or echo of our world. It is a place with decay and death. A plane out of phase, a place with monsters. It is right next to you and you don't even see it." *Dustin: reading the Dungeons & Dragons handbook.*

■ The second explorer after Vecna, Will described the Upside Down: "It's like home but it's so dark and empty and it's cold."

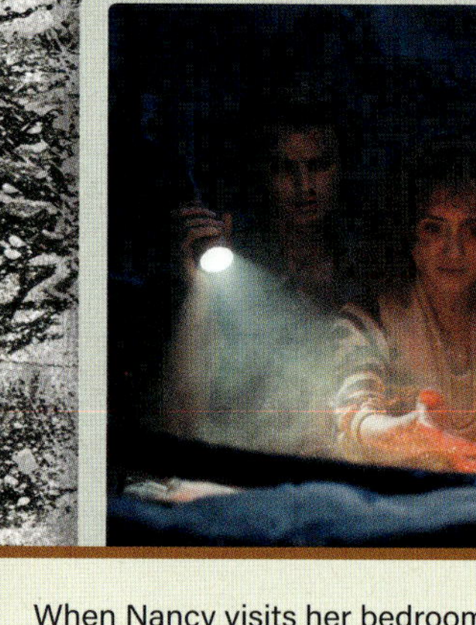

When Nancy visits her bedroom in the Upside Down, it's frozen in time on the day her brother's best friend disappeared, 6th November 1983? What does it all mean?

As Eleven killed the Demogorgon in 1983, she was sucked into the Upside Down and presumed missing or, worse, dead. She used her powers to find her way out.

"There's another world. A world hidden beneath Hawkins. Sometimes it bleeds into ours."

Dustin

When Vecna takes a life, it opens up a gate to the Upside Down. After Vecna killed Patrick, a gate opened up in Lover's Lake, christened 'Watergate' by Dustin. Steve took the plunge and dived down to take a closer look and was sucked into Vecna's world. FYI it was pretty dry on the flip side.

Steve's pool didn't have any water in when Barb found herself in it either. Is H_2O scarce in The Upside Down? So many questions!

In 1979, after Eleven pushed Henry Creel into the Upside Down, she stood and watched as the rift closed behind him, then forgot about it. Well, wouldn't you?

The Upside Down might be a peaceful place to chill out if it wasn't for all the vines everywhere sending something with teeth to come and find you, everytime you step on one! Stupid hive mind, spoiling everything as usual.

THE HAWKINS KIDS CALL THE OTHER WORLD 'THE UPSIDE DOWN' BUT THE US GOVERNMENT ORIGINALLY CALLED IT DIMENSION X.

The electromagnetic connection between our world and the Upside Down is strong. Compass needles readjust from pointing North, to pointing towards the gates. Electrically charged particles in one world affect light in the other. Joyce first discovered this when trying to communicate with Will. The gang used it again to send messages to each other.

HOW FAR DOES THE UPSIDE DOWN EXTEND? IS IT JUST HAWKINS? IMAGINE IF THERE WAS AN ENTIRE UPSIDE DOWN UNIVERSE. NOW, THAT'S SOME ARGYLE THINKING, DUDE.

STRANGER WORLDS

THE CREEL HOUSE

What went down at the Hawkins dream house was quickly transformed into the stuff of nightmares.

HOUSE FACTS

Location: The Creel House, Hawkins.

Built: 1800s.

Residents: Victor, Virginia, Alice and Henry Creel.

Massacre date: 14th March 1959.

Killed: Virginia and Alice.

Victor Creel moved to Hawkins with his family in 1959, hoping to make a fresh start for his troubled and sensitive son, Henry. Spoiler: it didn't work.

Henry's younger sister, Alice, loved her new home. "It looks like a fairytale. A dream."

Henry Creel was a strange young boy, who befriended deadly black widow spiders and discovered that he had unique abilities. He could move things with his mind and implant thoughts into other people's minds. His father never suspected his son was the malevolent cause of the weird goings-on in his home, putting it down to demons, the spawn of Satan, that sort of thing.

"We had one month of peace in that house, then it began."

Victor Creel

Henry terrorised his mum and sister, giving them horrible visions, before killing them both in the most gruesome manner – snapping their bones and removing their eyes. He would've killed his dad too, but he was too weak and passed out after two kills.

With his son in a coma, Victor Creel was wrongly arrested for the murder of his wife and daughter and imprisoned in Penhurst Mental Hospital, where he remained for decades.

Trawling through newspaper archives, Nancy and Robin discovered The Creel House's gruesome history. The intrepid pair posed as psychology students and paid a visit to Victor Creel.

After Max accidentally wandered into Vecna's personal space in his 'Mindscape', she spotted a distinctive front door with an unmistakable glass rose motif. Nancy remembered this from the clippings about the Victor Creel massacre. This was the first clue that Vecna and the Creel House were linked.

In 1986, the gang went to The Creel House to investigate. Steve was not a fan. "Yeah, that's not creepy."

They removed the boarding, revealing the rose door, which Robin swiftly broke through using a brick.

Dream a little Creel: Vecna's red soup version of his childhood home.

"He's a real bogeyman."

Wayne Munson on Victor Creel

THE FIRST TIME 'THE GANG' HEARD ABOUT THE CREEL FAMILY WAS WHEN EDDIE'S UNCLE WAYNE RECOUNTED A TOWN LEGEND, ABOUT THE DAD WHO KILLED HIS FAMILY AND REMOVED THEIR EYES. WHICH EDDIE HAD SEEN WITH CHRISSY. VERY SCARY. VERY SUSS. VERY NOT A COINCIDENCE.

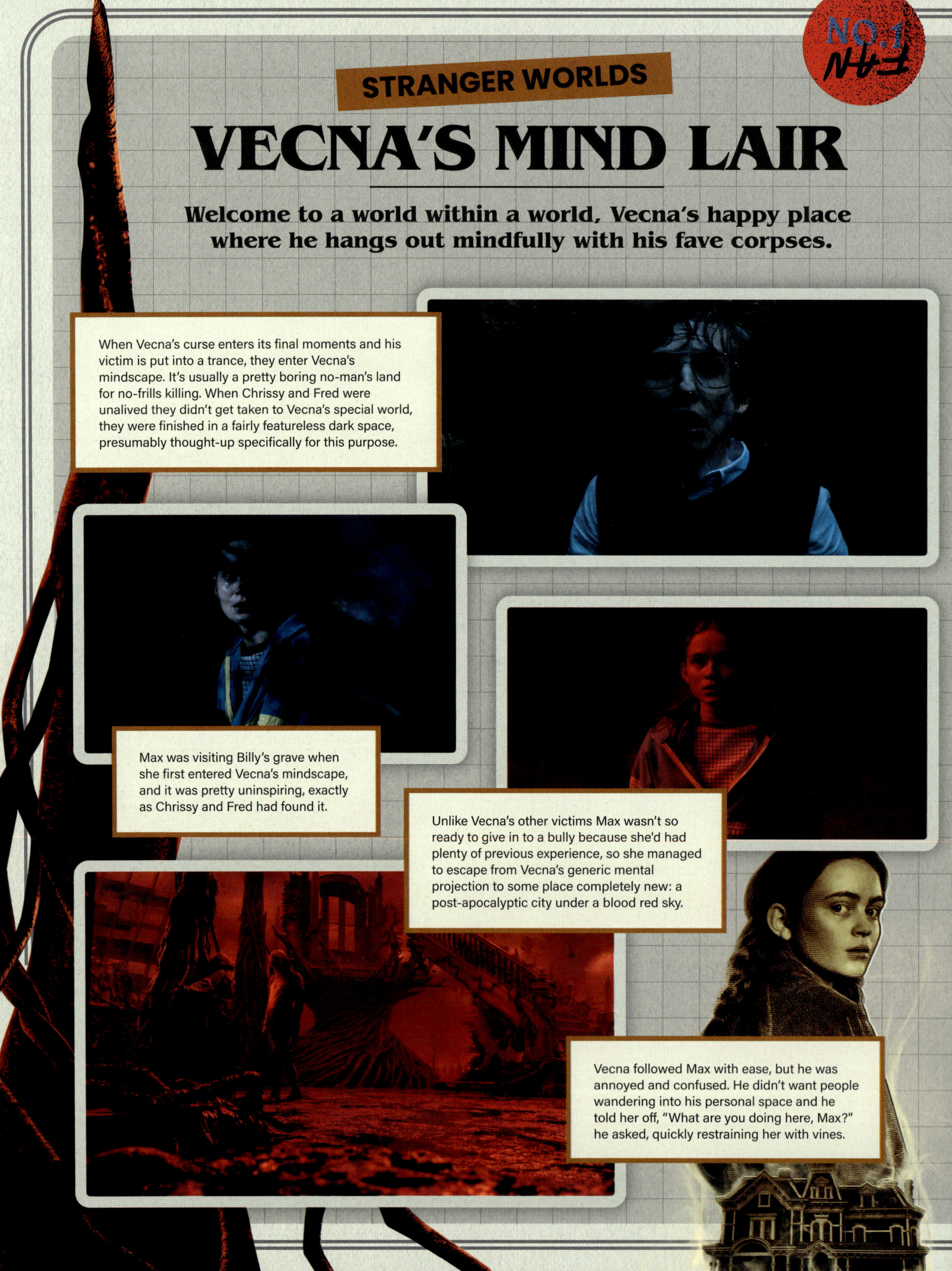

STRANGER WORLDS

VECNA'S MIND LAIR

Welcome to a world within a world, Vecna's happy place where he hangs out mindfully with his fave corpses.

When Vecna's curse enters its final moments and his victim is put into a trance, they enter Vecna's mindscape. It's usually a pretty boring no-man's land for no-frills killing. When Chrissy and Fred were unalived they didn't get taken to Vecna's special world, they were finished in a fairly featureless dark space, presumably thought-up specifically for this purpose.

Max was visiting Billy's grave when she first entered Vecna's mindscape, and it was pretty uninspiring, exactly as Chrissy and Fred had found it.

Unlike Vecna's other victims Max wasn't so ready to give in to a bully because she'd had plenty of previous experience, so she managed to escape from Vecna's generic mental projection to some place completely new: a post-apocalyptic city under a blood red sky.

Vecna followed Max with ease, but he was annoyed and confused. He didn't want people wandering into his personal space and he told her off, "What are you doing here, Max?" he asked, quickly restraining her with vines.

"Vecna's red soup mind world."

Steve

In the real world, Nancy and Robin discovered that music might have saved Victor Creel from his son's curse, so the gang place Max's headphones on her head and hit play on her favourite song, 'Running Up that Hill' by Kate Bush. This causes a cognitive break in Max's brain, reconnecting her brain to her body. She sees a portal to escape. As Kate sings about 'swapping places', Max's mind flees Vecna's Lair and her unconscious floating body crashes back to the ground – alive and herself again.

By the time Nancy was pulled into Vecna's Mindscape, he seemed to be less picky about letting her roam through his big red crib. At first, she was trapped in the pool that Barb was found dead in, but she instinctively climbed out.

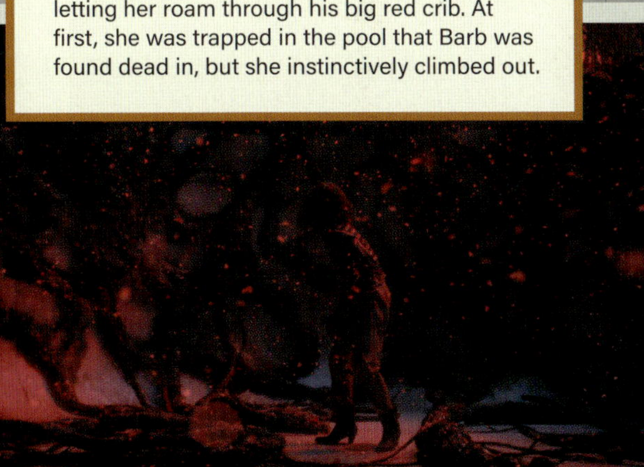

Then, Nancy somehow found herself on a floating staircase from the Creel House. Egotistical villain that he is, Vecna likely appreciated Nancy getting so close to working out the secret of his origin story. So, he indulged her investigative spirit by allowing her to enter his childhood memories, the same way Eleven had done with Billy. Eventually, he let her go. Looks like someone has a crush.

MINDSCAPE ... MORE LIKE HELLSCAPE

Vecna's Mind Lair exists on the ethereal plane of imagination. It's therefore built with Vecna's particular aesthetic choices: desolate and scary, misty, red and dark like the images of hell he probably saw as a child. He keeps his victims there as trophies trapped inside trees of vines, but there are fragments from his subconscious there too: fractured parts of his childhood house in Hawkins, the door, the staircase and its, frankly disturbing, grandfather clock.

OMG Gnarly!

THE CLOCK THAT CHIMES THE HOUR OF YOUR DEATH

When a mysterious clock appears, the countdown to your ding-donging death has begun.

Origin story

■ Henry Creel/001/Vecna was pushed into the Upside Down in 1979 and was alone there for four years. In his mind he constructed, or rather, deconstructed his house, along with its **ominous chiming grandfather clock**. Why is this so important? He told Eleven that life as we know it is basically a waste of time, "A cruel, oppressive world dictated by made-up rules. Seconds, minutes, hours, days, weeks, months, years, decades." Blah, blah, blah. So emo. But let's be real, the biggest reason Vecna signals his arrival with the ominous chimes of a clock is because he's a dramatic and cruel egomaniac who wants to enjoy the escalating panic in his victims.

WARNING:
If you hear the clock chime four times, it signals that your time is up. Some people believe that the four chimes were a clue pointing to Vecna's plan to open four gates to the Upside Down.

"It's just a clock, right?"
Robin

■ Cheer up, Chrissy!

Clockwatcher 1: Chrissy

■ Cheerleader Chrissy is the first victim of Vecna's curse and the **first person to have visions of his clock out in the woods**. Chrissy spots the clock nestling in a tree when she meets with Eddie. She doesn't understand its significance, but it's obviously not good.

Clockwatcher 2: Fred

■ When Fred went to investigate Chrissy's death with Nancy, little did he know that he was next on the chopping block. **Vecna's clock appears to Fred in the form of a coffin.** The creepiest apparition yet.

■ Tick tock killer clock

■ Safety in numbers?

Clockwatcher 3: Patrick

■ **Patrick did his best to hide his visions from his teammates**, so Vecna's curse came like a bolt out of the blue, taking devastating effect over Lover's Lake.

Clockwatcher 4: Max

■ When the school bell rings it's normally a good thing, but not for Max. **When she sees and hears Vecna's grandfather clock chiming it's sickly bing-bong**, it marks not the end of the school day, but the end – full stop.

■ School suddenly got worse

■ Time's almost up

Nancy's near miss

■ Nancy is about to leave the Upside Down with Steve, Robin and Eddie, when **Vecna snatches her conscious mind and drags it to his own Mindscape.** Under the spell of Vecna, Nancy enters his memories, finding herself transported back to the Creel House. She sees young Henry Creel with the dastardly grandfather clock that stands as an emblem of rigid rules and wasted time.

TRAINING TEST

LOOKOUT WITH LUCAS

Lucas is on a mission, but he dropped his trusty binoculars and now they're badly cracked. Can you help him figure out who or what he's seeing, and more importantly if he should RUN AWAY because you're both in danger, GO SAY HI because you're safe, or SIT & WAIT to gather more intel.

WHAT TO DO:

Write the name of who or what you think is in the picture and circle the action you would take. Think carefully, because this could mean life or y'know – the other thing.

1

WHO OR WHAT: ....

GO SAY HI • RUN AWAY • SIT & WAIT

2

WHO OR WHAT: ....

AND ....

GO SAY HI • RUN AWAY • SIT & WAIT

3

WHO OR WHAT: ....

GO SAY HI • RUN AWAY • SIT & WAIT

4

WHO OR WHAT: ....

GO SAY HI • RUN AWAY • SIT & WAIT

5

WHO OR WHAT: ....

GO SAY HI • RUN AWAY • SIT & WAIT

6

WHO OR WHAT: ....

GO SAY HI • RUN AWAY • SIT & WAIT

ANSWERS ON PAGE 118

TRAINING TEST

SPOT THE DIFFERENCE

How different is the Upside Down from the 'real world'? No one can say. How many differences can you find in the Upside Down picture below?

TICK A BOX FOR EVERY DIFFERENCE YOU FIND.

ANSWERS ON PAGE 118

STRANGER CREATURES

VECNA

This villain is the #1 worst thing in the world – and he's not even in our world, well, he wasn't ...

HENRY CREEL

Vecna was never ordinary. As a little boy he made friends with deadly spiders and killed his family. He had special powers so Dr Brenner at Hawkins Lab was very interested in his abilities.

001

Dr Brenner kept Henry/001 under control whilst trying to replicate his powers in children who weren't as murderous. But when Henry got the chance he killed again. When Eleven stopped him she did so with such a force of power that she sent him into another dimension.

VECNA'S EVOLUTION

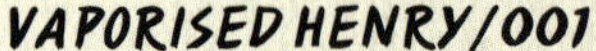

VAPORISED HENRY/001

In the alternate dimension, Henry was like – 'I've found my spiritual home.' A place unspoiled by mankind, just weird particles of living matter that he could fashion into monstrous beings - such as the spider-like Mind Flayer.

VECNA

For years he lived there - becoming one with the life forms. Fusing into them, combining his atoms with theirs. It was fun for a while - but when Eleven opened a gate to the Upside Down in 1983, Henry or Vecna, as he would be known, decided that it might be cool to make our world more like his.

DEAD TEENS OPEN GATES

Upside Down dwellers taking lives from our right-way-up world opens a rift between the two and Vecna loved that idea. He began killing off unhappy teenagers. He planned to open four portals which would join up, to make a super-giant rift between the worlds so that his monsters could devour the earth and deadly spores would kill all living things. Chrissy was first, then Fred and Patrick.

"An undead creature of great power ... a dark wizard."

Dustin

MAD MAX

Vecna's last victim for his 4-portal-plan was Max Mayfield, a bad choice because she had very powerful friends, including his old foe Eleven.

TRAPPED IN HIS OWN WEB

When the Hellfire Club discovered Vecna was connecting psychically with his victims, they realised his body must stay behind in the Upside Down, specifically in the attic of the Creel House. Suspended from vines, Vecna resembled the deadly spiders he admired so much. He looked cool, but while he was catching prey from within his hive-mind 'web', he was also vulnerable to attack.

OH SNOW YOU DON'T

Max coaxed Vecna to come and get her, hoping to escape from his Mind Lair to her own Mindscape, a happier place where she would be safe. She chose the Snowball, where she first danced with Lucas. But Vecna was no dummy, he found her, and even when Eleven turned up to help, he couldn't be stopped.

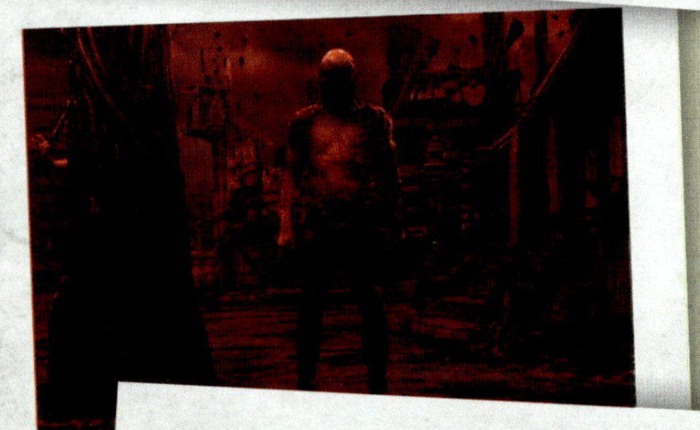

C'MON RED

Vecna regained control, dragging Eleven and Max to his murky red Mind Lair.

4 WAYS TO KILL VECNA: A BRAINSTORM

- MAX
  STAKE THROUGH HEART!
- EDDIE
  BULLET!
- LUCAS
  CHOP OFF HEAD!
- NANCY
  ALL OF THE ABOVE!

FINAL STAND

As Eleven battled Vecna's mind in the Mindscape, Steve, Nancy and Robin snuck into the Upside Down, found his body in the attic and set fire to it. Nancy shot him out of the window, but when they ran downstairs, his body was gone. Bloody typical!

Vecna's Curse

Before Vecna takes the life of a person he begins to infiltrate their mind. Because of this they start to suffer a series of symptoms:

- Headaches
- Nightmares
- Waking up in a cold sweat
- Reliving past traumas
- Terrifying visions
- Entering a trance
- Being lifted into the air
- Bones twisting and snapping
- Eyes removed
- Death

001 VS 011: ROUND 3!

Vecna's original plan had been for Eleven to join him in his global annihilation. In a way she was his spiritual sister, but Eleven could never join him, she is NOT a monster like him. It took her a while to figure that out, but she got there. Pinned against the front door of The Creel House in Vecna's Mind Lair, she listened to his long and twisted story.

ALL YOU NEED IS LOVE

Vecna told Eleven to watch him kill Max. Eleven was crushed and felt utterly powerless. Only a massive dose of love could defeat this much cruelty. And so, in the real world, Mike told her that he loved her and to: "Fight. Fight. Fight," she heard him and that's exactly what she did.

DEMOGORGON 1983

STRANGER CREATURES

THE DEMOGORGON

When the mysterious monster from another world arrived it shot straight to the top of the food chain.

NAME

The Demogorgon does not have an officially recognised name. It goes by the nickname given to it by the young members of the Dungeons & Dragons club, because in that game, there's a fierce monster called the Demogorgon.

HABITAT

The creature lives in a desolate, dark and hostile world once simply known as Dimension X, but now dubbed, 'the Upside Down'.

PHYSIOLOGY

The vaguely humanoid fully-grown adult is between six and ten feet tall, with long, slender, bony limbs and a head that unfolds like the petals of a deadly flower, filled with rows and rows of razor-sharp teeth.

ABILITIES

The Demogorgon is a strong, super-fast, ruthless hunter, with an excellent sense of smell (able to detect spilled blood) and able to travel across dimensions killing prey and opening portals between worlds with ease.

ДЕМОГОРГОН

MON
STER

FIRST CONTACT

Eleven first encountered a Demogorgon when she was in The Void, spying on a Russian agent for Dr Brenner. That time she merely heard the terrifying sound of its snarling. When she went back into The Void to track it, she reached out and touched the monster, and inadvertently created a gate between worlds.

FIRST OUTING

After Eleven had accidentally opened the gateway to the Upside Down in East Hawkins, one of its most ferocious predators, the Demogorgon, slipped through, hunting for something to eat.

FIRST SNATCHING

The Demogorgon's first victim was Will Byers, who it snatched and took back to its home to save for later. Will was thankfully rescued by his mum, Joyce, and Chief Hopper.

FIRST KILL

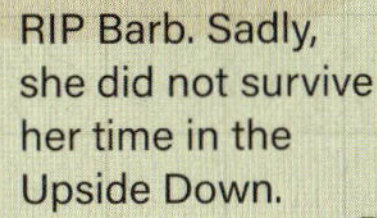

RIP Barb. Sadly, she did not survive her time in the Upside Down.

LURING IT

After it killed her BFF, Nancy wanted revenge. So, she and Jonathan set a trap for the Demogorgon by luring it with blood.

KILLING IT

Eleven kills the Demogorgon with her telekinetic powers, splitting it into smithereens.

FIRST SIGHTING, ON FILM

In a photograph of Barbara Holland on the diving board of Steve Harrington's pool, taken by Jonathan Byers right before the creature snatched Barb and dragged her to the Upside Down.

FIRST SIGHTING IRL

Nancy and Jonathan witnessed a Demogorgon feeding on a deer. Ew!

The life stages of a Demogorgon

The science isn't rigorous at this point, but this is what has been observed.

1. **The larval stage.** Demogorgons seem to hatch out of dead bodies. Barb had one inside her and Will threw up a slug-like thing, which may or may not have been a first stage Demogorgon.
2. **Polywog/tadpole.** This is the deceptively cute, palm-sized form in which Dustin discovers his 'pet', D'Artagnan, otherwise known as Dart.
3. **Frogogorgon.** When Dart was growing up he sprouted back legs, but had yet to exhibit the toothed flower-face associated with the evolved Demogorgon.
4. **Catogorgon.** When Dart breaks out of his cage and devours Dustin's beloved cat, Mews, he's about the size of a large cat and has the petal-opening head of teeth.
5. **Demodog/Dogogorgon.** The penultimate stage of transition, the last four-legged stage. Hawkins Lab was overrun with a vast number of Demodogs at this stage.
6. **Demogorgon.** Upright creature that can now come face to face with you as it devours your face with its face.

I ♥ DEMOCORGONS

STRANGER CREATURES

TOP 5 MONSTERS TO KEEP YOU UP AT NIGHT

Each year something more terrifying emerges out of the dark in Hawkins, but which is the worst?

Mind Flayer

Mind Flayer	
Size: Unknown, but at least as massive as a football pitch.	10/10
Power: Possibly the most powerful creature in the Upside Down.	10/10
Gross-rating: It's a more mental than visual fear.	5/10
Terror factor: It's crushing need to destroy is pretty horrific.	9/10
Agility: Through the servants of the Hive Mind it can strike quite swiftly.	7/10
Intelligence: The Mind Flayer is the architect of many mean schemes. Kudos, baddie.	9/10

SPECIAL MOVE

Getting everyone else to do its dirty work.

FIND IT...

Lurking over schools and stalking Will Byers.

Spider Monster

Spider Monster	
Size: Huge, at least two storeys high	9/10
Power: With all of the Mind Flayer's essence fuelling it, a lot.	9/10
Gross-rating: Those tenacle suckers are especially yuck. The whole beast is pretty hideous.	9/10
Terror factor: Its giant mouth and the sheer size of it are pee-in-your-pants scary.	8/10
Agility: Anything this huge can't move fast, but its tentacles are sneaky and swift.	7/10
Intelligence: As clever as it is evil.	8/10

SPECIAL MOVE

Sucking the life out of a person.

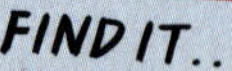

FIND IT...

In the mall or the steelworks.

Hospital Monster

SPECIAL MOVE

Dissolving at a moment's notice and slipping under doors and into drains.

FIND IT ...

Duh, in hospitals.

Size: Big! The width of a corridor.	7/10
Power: It's controlled by the Mind Flayer – so its own power is not that massive.	6/10
Gross-rating: This thing is hideous beyond words.	10/10
Terror factor: See it, and you WILL have nightmares.	9/10
Agility: It can get into every crack and cranny, but it does lumber somewhat.	6/10
Intelligence: Not dumb, but not the Einstein of flesh-lumps either.	5/10

ОБРАЗЕЦ: ДЕМОБАТ

1st Finger

2nd Finger

SPECIAL MOVE

Swooping out of nowhere and biting.

FIND IT ...

In the blood red skies of the Upside Down.

Demobat

Size: Pretty titchy.	3/10
Power: Their power is in numbers.	5/10
Gross-rating: The fact they live in the dark, means we never get a proper look at them – phew!	5/10
Terror factor: A killer swarm is no walk in the mall as Eddie found out.	7/10
Agility: These little killers are nimble as anything in the Upside Down.	9/10
Intelligence: Low. As foot-soldiers (wing-soldiers?) of the Hive Mind, they rely on their 'programming.'	4/10

Russian Demogorgon

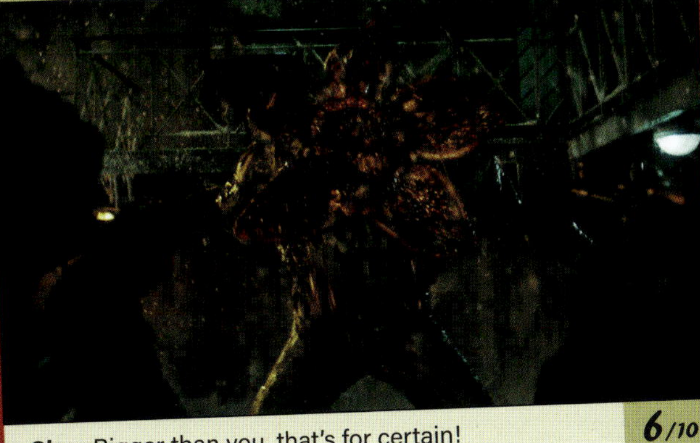

Size: Bigger than you, that's for certain!	6/10
Power: They're incredibly strong. Never fight one, always run.	8/10
Gross-rating: They are more awe-inspiring than vom-inducing.	6/10
Terror factor: As soon as they open their petal-head to reveal endless rows of teeth, it's over.	10/10
Agility: Fast as lightning and just as dextrous.	10/10
Intelligence: These Hive Mind monsters seem to have a mind of their own.	8/10

SPECIAL MOVE

Opening its wretched flower face to devour you.

FIND IT ...

In a cage waiting to eat you.

DEMOGORGON 1983

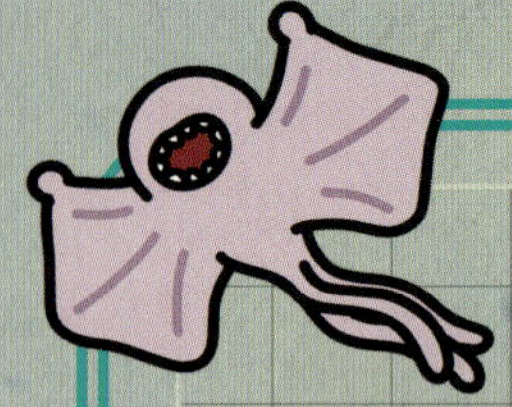

TRAINING TEST

SEARCH AND DESTROY

Find the 18 bad things in this wordsearch, cross them out and consider them ... eradicated.

P	H	H	E	S	Y	A	N	G	E	L	A	R	L
H	M	S	G	N	D	E	M	O	B	A	T	D	O
D	E	C	V	E	V	V	S	P	O	R	E	S	N
V	E	Z	S	A	E	P	I	V	E	L	E	D	N
R	R	M	C	H	C	Y	E	N	W	I	N	M	I
H	A	F	O	G	N	L	K	O	E	Z	O	O	E
T	E	L	Z	G	A	T	E	S	B	S	S	A	B
D	G	A	M	Z	O	O	V	W	I	T	E	Z	Y
E	R	Y	D	K	D	R	H	S	L	M	B	O	E
L	I	E	J	A	U	X	G	O	L	P	L	R	R
Y	G	D	A	R	C	L	C	O	Y	A	E	I	S
I	O	F	S	F	Z	H	T	D	N	P	E	S	X
N	R	Z	O	N	T	O	E	R	Y	A	D	K	Y
G	I	E	N	W	N	O	G	S	A	I	S	S	J

ANGELA
DEMOBAT
DEMOGORGON
FLAYED
BILLY
GATES
HEADACHES
JASON
VINES
LYING
MK ULTRA
LONNIE BYERS
NOSEBLEEDS
PAPA
RISKS
SPORES
VECNA
GRIGORI

ANSWERS ON PAGE 118

DEMO-DRAW-GON

The Hawkins police chief has asked you draw the flower-faced beast that dragged Barb into Steve's pool, who Nancy and Jonathan saw and Eleven even pinned to a wall. Grab a pencil or a pen and hop to it (no pun intended.)

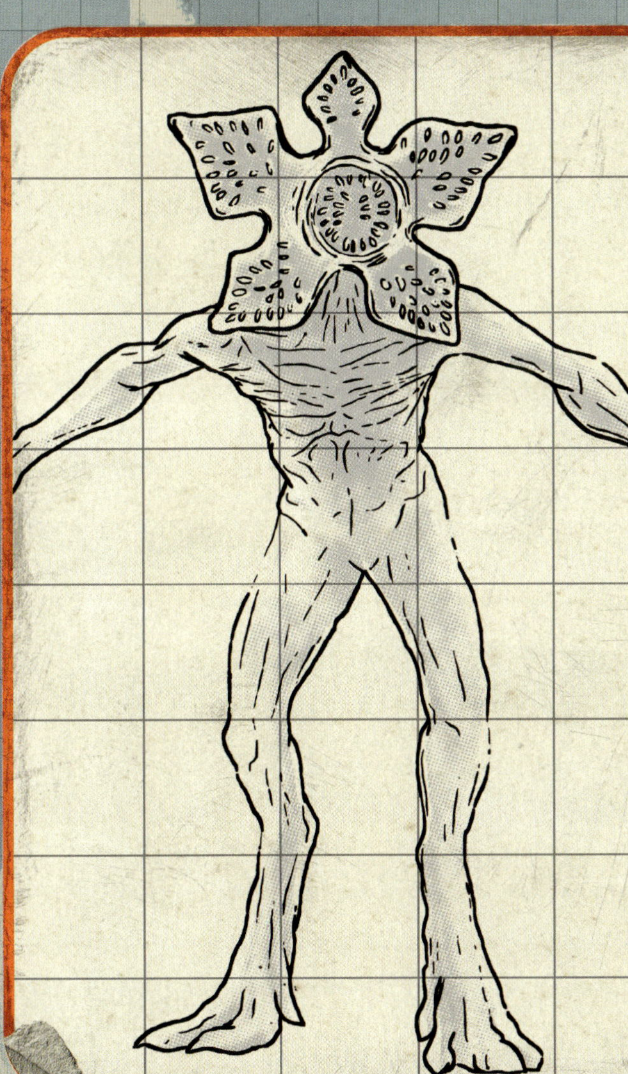

EVERY GOOD INVESTIGATOR NEEDS TO BE ABLE TO RECORD THEIR FINDINGS IN AS MUCH DETAIL AS POSSIBLE.

EVEN ROUGH SKETCHES CAN BE VALUABLE SOURCES OF INFORMATION.

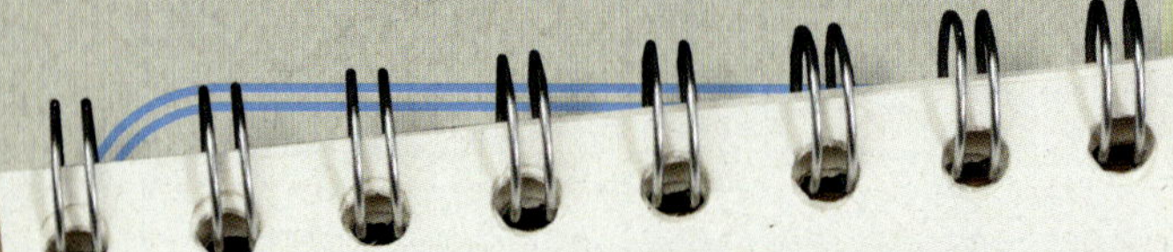

A SNAPSHOT OF A VERY STRANGE

HAWKINS

19 83

When a kid goes missing, his friends and family aren't about to sit around and do nothing. Their journey of discovery is long, and filled with monsters, bad men and an unbelievable amount of chocolate pudding. Like, who is hoarding this much pudding? But I digress ...

■ How it started ...

■ On his cycle home Will Byers gets snatched and taken to another realm. After a session of coffee and contemplation, Detective Jim Hopper finds Will's bike and an official investigation begins.

HAVE YOU SEEN ME?

Will Byers Aged 12 4'9"
Brown Hair, Brown Eyes, 73lbs
Last seen wearing: Jeans,
Blue Plaid Shirt, White T-Shirt.
Red Down Vest with tan stripe.
Carrying Black Canvas Day Bag.
Any information call Joyce Byers
555 7941

■ The Party discover a girl in the rain. The girl tells Mike, Dustin and Lucas that her name is Eleven. Mike lets her stay his basement in his den.

■ Eleven explains that Will has been taken to the Upside Down by showing the boys the underside of their Dungeons & Dragons game board. Will is hiding from the Demogorgon there.

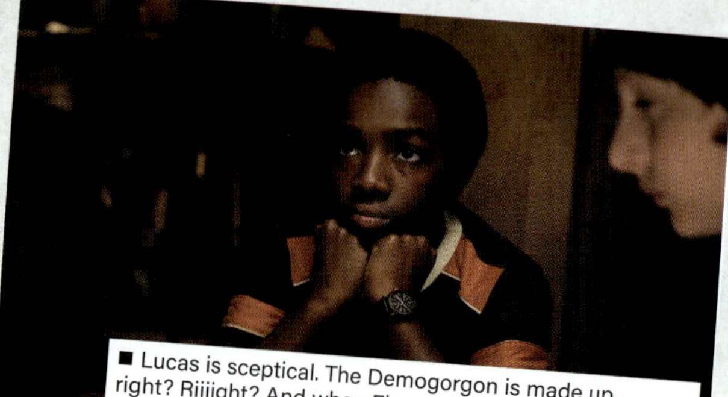

■ Lucas is sceptical. The Demogorgon is made up, right? Riiiight? And when El reveals her powers, Lucas is all like: "She's not a superhero. She's a weirdo."

Hawkins Middle School A.V. CLUB

Barb should never have agreed to go to Steve's with Nancy.

■ El tries to contact Will through the walkie talkie, but it doesn't work. It isn't powerful enough.

■ They need to get Eleven to the ham radio at school, which is powerful enough to reach Australia, so maybe it can handle a near-ish dimension. El puts on a disguise so that "the bad men" that she's running from won't find her.

■ "The bad men" have kept Eleven locked up her whole life, in a special facility where they try to harness her powers for secret government projects.

■ The boys think that they are the only ones trying to find Will. But when Mike's sister, Nancy, contacts the gang, they soon discover that Hopper and Joyce, and Jonathan and Nancy, are on their side and have been searching for Will just like they have.

■ Nancy has been to the Upside Down and hated it. She hatches a plan with Will's brother Jonathan to kill the Demogorgon once and for all.

■ While Nancy, Steve and Jonathan kill one Demogorgon at the Byers' house, Eleven faces another at the school ...

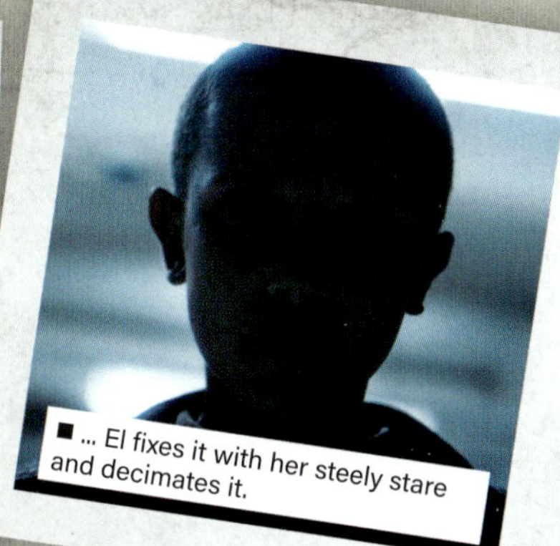
■ ... El fixes it with her steely stare and decimates it.

■ Will is found and rescued by Joyce and Hoppe and brought back to our world. Everything looks like it's back to normal ...

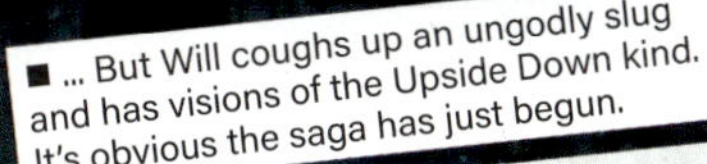
■ ... But Will coughs up an ungodly slug and has visions of the Upside Down kind. It's obvious the saga has just begun.

Chatting with fairy lights is the best communication innovation since since, er, ham radio.

LEAVING HAWKINS ... AGAIN SOON

CLOSE UP ON ...

THE HAWKINS TUNNEL SYSTEM

Or ... How the Upside Down burrows into town!

Between our world and the Upside Down lies a subterranean network of tunnels: the Hawkins Tunnel System. Hundreds of secret passages reaching out from the Upside Down to cause as much harm as possible.

Something rotten

■ Reports of dying crops sent Chief Hopper on an investigation all over Hawkins. **Plants, trees, vegetables, everything was decaying – in a really gross way.** This was obviously more than a vindictive rivalry between farmers or a Halloween prank.

Hopper in the burrow

■ Hopper dug into the ground, found an opening into the tunnels and went to explore. What the police chief didn't realise was that the tunnels were not only twisty, confusing and easy to get lost in, they were also alive and deadly. When Hopper was sprayed in the face with spores he was knocked unconscious.

Will the Wise

■ Will had been 'possessed' by the Mind Flayer, which meant that he remained part of the hive mind that connects all the creatures of the Upside Down like a single organism – and that included the tunnel system.

At first this was a good thing. Will mapped out all of the tunnels, scribbling everything he could see in his 'now memories' without really understanding what it was he was seeing. Joyce realised that the pictures he drew connected and she started to join them together sticking them all over the walls of her living room.

WHAT ARE THE TUNNELS?

The tunnels are ... **alive**

The tunnels are ... **part of a hive mind connected directly to the Mind Flayer**

The tunnels are ... **not filled with clean safe air to breathe**

The tunnels are ... **crawling with sentient vines**

The tunnels are ... **out to get you**

Steve the firestarter

■ Steve was against having a gang of children under his protection going into the tunnels to start a fire, but there was no stopping them, so he joined them. The idea was to lure the Demodogs away from the Lab giving Eleven time to close the gate to the Upside Down.

■ Not sure how much use goggles and a bandanna over the face were to protect against the noxious spores, but they seemed to help.

Will to the rescue

■ Will has a vision of Hopper passed out underground in his 'now memories.' Thanks to her son, Joyce Byers had a map of the tunnels but couldn't work out where Hopper was. But Bob Newby could. He realised that the tunnels fit over the layout and landmarks of Hawkins and Joyce went to rescue Hopper.

"I think he's going to die."

Will

PLACES BOB NEWBY IDENTIFIED ON WILL'S MAP OF THE TUNNELS:

- **Lover's Lake**
- **Lake Jordan**
- **The Sattler quarry**
- **The Eno River**

■ All those cute little particles that look like fairy dust or snowflakes are actually highly poisonous.

WHAT IS THE HUB?

The hub of the tunnel system was where many of the tunnels met. It was also a sort of graveyard filled with bones.

■ Will's drawing of the Hawkins tunnels.

RIP Dart

■ The gang are making their way to the hub to splash petrol everywhere and set the place on fire, when they meet Dustin's pet Demodog, Dart. Dart doesn't eat Dustin, he eats a chocolate bar instead, allowing Dustin and his friends to pass safely and set fire to the tunnel system. Little does Dart realise that by doing that he was sacrificing himself for his friend.

"It's been spreading, growing beneath us, like some cancer."

Dr Owens on the tunnel system

WARNING: Demodogs don't make good pets!

OMG Gnarly!

DART: THE PET THAT BIT BACK

When Dustin adopted a stray critter, he didn't expect it to grow up to be a literal hellhound!

Origin story

■ Dustin found Dart, an orphaned wiggly creature in a dustbin. **He called him D'Artagnan** after a character in the story of The Three Musketeers because he fed the creature a 3 Musketeers chocolate bar and he seemed to like it. Dustin kept the tiny thing in his tortoise's tank, but it grew pretty fast and broke out.

PROFILE

Full name: D'Artagnan.
Nickname: Dart.
What it's not: Some little lizard. Some nasty slug.
What it is: A Demogorgon at growth stages 2-5, aka a Demodog.
Nature: Vicious predator.
Resembles: 'A living booger' (Lucas).
Feels: 'Slimy' (Max).
Likes: Digging, the dark, nougat, eating cats, luncheon meat.
Dislikes: Bright hot lights, basements.

"He doesn't bite."

Dustin (famous last words)

The gang have mixed feelings about Dart

Polliwog

■ Dustin Henderson is no slouch. The moment he found Dart, he wanted to know what he was. **After some careful research, Dustin deduced that he was a polliwog,** which is the term used for something like a tadpole which is the larval or intermediate stage of a bigger creature. Dustin got that right. What he didn't realise was that the slippery lump was the baby stage of a Demogorgon. Uh oh.

Bad Mews

■ When Dart started to grow up, he shed his skin and escaped his tank. All that activity made him peckish but without any candy, **he had to snack on the cat**. Had to. Poor Mews.

RIP Mews, you never stood a chance

This story did NOT have a happy ending

Show and tell

■ **Dustin took Dart to school. Dumb idea**. It escaped, but luckily Dustin caught it and hid it under his hat. Smart, or maybe not smart. He then lured/trapped it in his basement, but of course Dart dug his way out.

Killer advice

■ Trying to catch Dart isn't the best day out, but Dustin and Steve really bonded during this bloody activity, with **Steve tossing out valuable nuggets of dating advice** along with his raw chunks of meat. Like: "act like you don't care" and "wait until you feel it" before you make your move.

Hansel and Gretel could never

Tubular take-away

■ Monsters are made, not born. Dustin was a loving dad and that affected Dart in a good way. When they came face-to-face in the Hawkins Tunnel system, Dart let Dustin and his pals pass. **Even a creature under the evil influence of the Mind Flayer can show kindness**, if it is taught the value of being kind.

How to disable a Demodog

■ If you ever come face to face with a Demodog like Dart, wear protective clothing, like ice hockey gear, a helmet or cricket pads. Slow it down with the promise of ham slices and disable it with a hockey stick or baseball bat. Or you could try to appeal to its 'better nature.'

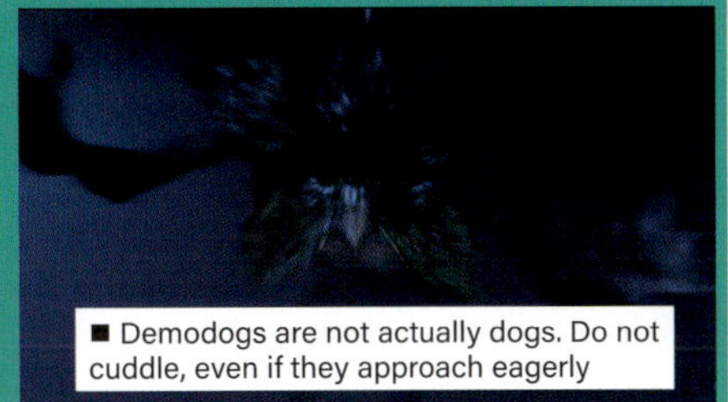

Demodogs are not actually dogs. Do not cuddle, even if they approach eagerly

TEST SUBJECT

WHICH CLIQUE WILL YOU PICK?

If you were going to join one of Hawkins' extra-curricular clubs, which one would it be? Take this test and find out.

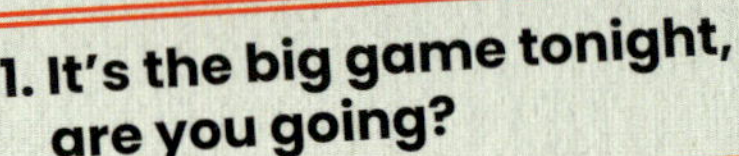

1. It's the big game tonight, are you going?

A - Hell yes! Team spirit for the win!
B - Hell no! I'm busy with that other thing
C - I would go (for a laugh), but I've got work
D - Nah, I'm just chilling

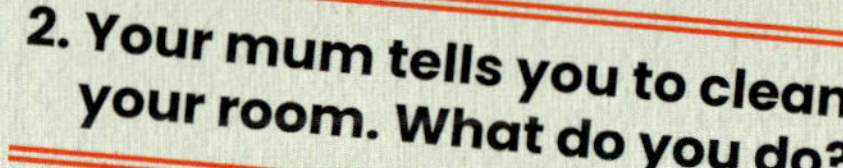

2. Your mum tells you to clean your room. What do you do?

A - Tell her it's already spotless and invite her to see
B - Yell that you'll do it later
C - Explain that mess is part of life, and to fight it is futile
D - Do what you're told

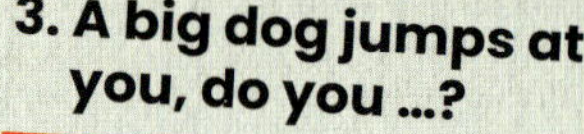

3. A big dog jumps at you, do you ...?

A - Get ready to fight
B - Run the hell away
C - Crouch and pet the little pup
D - Just stand there

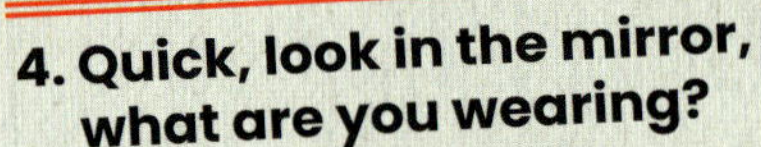

4. Quick, look in the mirror, what are you wearing?

A - Chinos and a polo shirt
B - Biker jacket, jeans, band tee
C - Something lame and comical, no doubt with a jaunty hat
D - Swimwear counts ... right?

MOSTLY As

Jason recruits you for the school basketball team, the Hawkins High Tigers.

You're a regular team player who can be a bit controlling at times and a bit too fond of the limelight. You're pretty active and healthy which is good, but winning isn't everything and maybe you should chill out and read a book every now and then.

MOSTLY Bs

Eddie Munson invites you to join the Hellfire D&D club.

You're something of an outsider, and that's good in these trying times. You're gonna need to think outside the pack, when they come growling at your door. Escapism into fantasy is fine, but remember to come up and get some air sometimes.

5. How would your granny describe you?

A - Her perfect golden boy/girl
B - A big disappointment
C - A little bit special
D - Missing

6. We're at the mall, where are you headed first?

A - To get the latest trainers
B - The exit, that corporate mess is shallow and expensive
C - The food court, no question
D - Anywhere with air con

7. The TV is on, what are we watching dude?

A - ThunderCats
B - The 1978 classic Lord of The Rings animation
C - A pirate copy of Fast Times at Ridgemont High on VHS
D - My reflection in the empty black screen

8. Pick your fave season

A - Spring
B - Summer
C - Autumn
D - Winter

9. Let's play a game. How long will it last?

A - Four 12-minute quarters
B - 10 hours at least
C - Game? What sort of game? Nothing nerdy, for no amount of time.
D - There's no time for games

10. Where do you have your best chats?

A - With a microphone and a room full of people listening
B - In the woods or the basement
C - Sitting on the floor of the bathroom at the mall
D - In my head

MOSTLY Cs

Steve and Robin hire you for Scoops Troop duty.

Some people are a conundrum – that's you. One minute deep and philosophical, the next a complete basketcase running your mouth off about some nonsense. Also, you need to eat healthier. Ice cream is not one of the essential food groups, you know!

MOSTLY Ds

Billy wants you to make up numbers for The Flayed.

Some call you a daydreamer, others say you're lazy. You are quite intense and in your head and tend to 'run a bit hot.' If you like the window open, even in November, then you've found your tribe. Expect some very close bonding sessions.

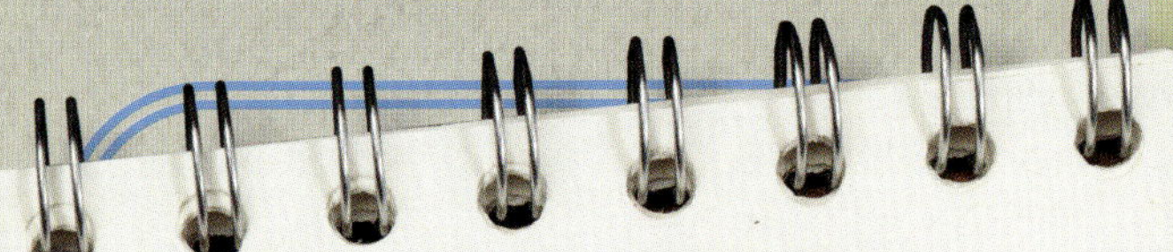

IT WAS ALL OUT WAR IN '84

The Upside Down starts to come at Hawkins sideways, burrowing under the town and into the brain and body of Will Byers.

■ After destroying the Demogorgon, El is transported to the Upside Down. Luckily, she spies an opening back into her world. Will her powers work on the gooey stringy fabric between worlds? Yes! She widens the hole to climb through and escapes.

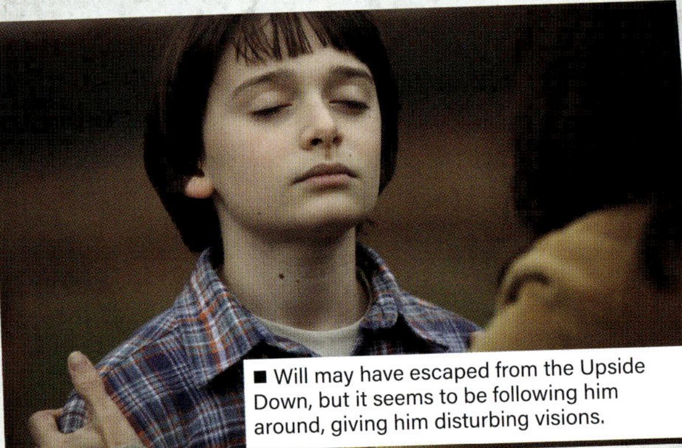

■ Will may have escaped from the Upside Down, but it seems to be following him around, giving him disturbing visions.

■ Halloween is approaching and Merill Wright's field of pumpkins have all turned black and rotten. The farmer thinks they're being poisoned by his vengeful neighbour, Eugene.

■ A new girl, Max and her brother Billy arrive in town. Max is a bit snarky at first, but she slowly pals-up with The Party – well Lucas and Dustin. Mike is less thrilled, he misses Eleven who's been gone for 352 days.

■ Eleven isn't actually missing, she's hiding out in Hopper's secret cabin in the woods. It's very boring: there's only so much TV and Eggos a girl can take – so she runs away.

■ At first El has a local walk about, then she goes on a road trip to find her mother and her 'sister.'

■ Hopper doesn't realise El is missing because he's too busy investigating dead pumpkins. This leads him to a series of tunnels under Hawkins, which turns out to be a refuge for some creepy murderous vines that trap him down there.

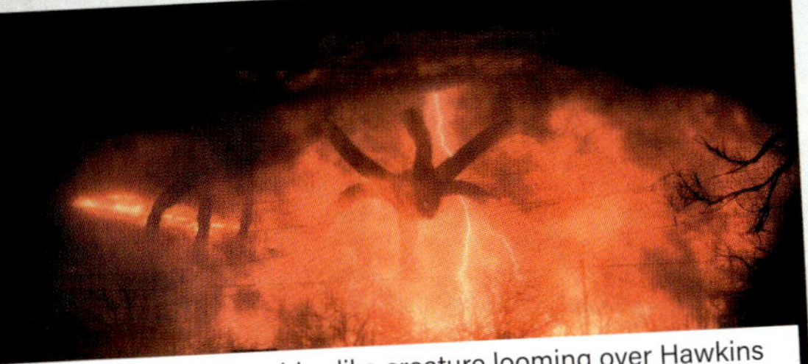

■ Will's visions of a spider-like creature looming over Hawkins get worse, which is bad enough. Then he gets possessed which is even worse. He isn't all bad yet though and thanks to his 'now memories' he lets everyone know they need to rescue Hopper.

■ Meanwhile Dustin has foolishly (or fortuitously?) adopted a baby Demogorgon he calls Dart. Dart grows fast and turns into an animal Dustin calls a Demodog. Dart is not a one-off and soon the horrifying creatures are terrorising the Hawkins Lab.

■ El finds her 'sister' Kali, in Chicago and the two bond. Kali escaped from The Hawkins Lab years before Eleven, and life on the streets has made her strong but ruthless. Kali teaches El to use her painful memories to turbo-charge her powers, which she's about to seriously need. A walk through The Void shows Mike in trouble so El returns to Hawkins to help.

■ Demodogs attack the Byers house, and although Nancy and the gang are ready to fight, Eleven shows up, does what she does and saves everyone from significant blood loss, not to mention hassle.

■ Eleven can't just clock off and go home. She has to go and shut the gate between worlds. It's the only way to drive the 'Mind Flayer,' as it's been called, out of Will and stop all the crazy stuff that's happening in Hawkins.

■ The Demodogs are swarming, so the gang think of a plan to get them away from Hawkins Lab to make it easier for El to go and shut the gate without having to use up her powers on 'canine' control. They mask-up and descend into the deadly tunnels to start a fire to lure the D-dogs there.

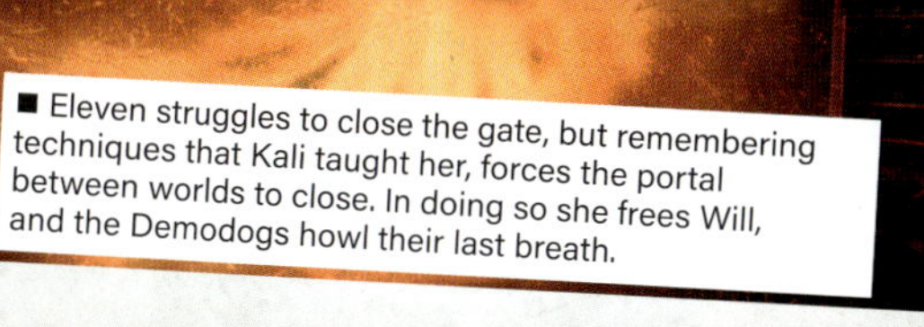

■ Eleven struggles to close the gate, but remembering techniques that Kali taught her, forces the portal between worlds to close. In doing so she frees Will, and the Demodogs howl their last breath.

■ The town returns to normal for a minute and the kids celebrate being kids with an old-fashioned school dance. Kissing ensues.

Snow Ball '84

BAD IDEA!

Smoking and weight-lifting is the dumbest thing since adopting a demon-dog. Billy you're the worst.

RAD IDEA!

Getting Bob 'The Brain' to work out what Will's drawings mean. Bob's the best.

CLOSE UP ON ...

THE SNOW BALL

The big blow out after Eleven closed the gate to the Upside Down was a night to remember.

DATE: 15 DECEMBER 1984
DRESS CODE: FANCY
THE PUNCH: PURE FUEL

You look like a million bucks

■ **Dustin took Steve's hair advice** and, well, this happened. Looking flash and filled with confidence, Dustin plucked up the courage to ask popular girl, Stacy, to dance. Sadly, she wasn't having any of it.

■ Is there a bird nesting in there?

DJ PLAYLIST

LOVE IS A BATTLEFIELD BY PAT BENATAR

TWIST OF FATE BY OLIVIA NEWTON JOHN

TIME AFTER TIME BY CYNDI LAUPER

EVERY BREATH YOU TAKE BY THE POLICE

■ A reminder that Will is a tiny child who's suffered more than any tiny child should

So smooth, Lucas

■ The traumatic events of the past months **brought the gang closer together than ever**. Like really close. Lucas and Max had their first kiss and even Will had an awkward side-to-side with a random admirer. Dustin, however didn't have as much luck.

You look beautiful

■ The Snow Ball is a school dance, which means that you have to dance, something Mike and Eleven do not feel they can do. They didn't let that stop them though, with Mike suggesting: **"Do you wanna figure it out?"** (spoiler alert, they figured it out).

TOLD YOU SO!

Mike told Eleven that he'd wanted to take her to the Snow Ball way back in 1983.

Nancy to the rescue

■ Nancy spots Dustin having a rubbish time alone on the bleachers while his friends get their smooch on. "Wanna dance?" she says. "Come on!" She pulls him to his feet and **the little dude has never looked happier**. As Nancy guides him around the dance floor, stuck up Stacy looks gobsmacked.

Getting their smooch on

■ **Mike and Eleven kiss**, something they would continue to do daily – until the intervention of Hopper half a year later.

Snow Ball '84

■ The Snow Ball was a such a happy night for Max, that in 1986 when she was being pursued by Vecna, she chose her memory of the event to hide from him ...

■ ... But Vecna is well aware of the Snow Ball. Max couldn't have known this, but Vecna's ally-in-evil, the mysterious Mind Flayer was watching over the event.

■ When El shows up in Max's memory of the Snow Ball she can't believe it. It is in fact very confusing, but apparently Eleven can insert herself into the memories of other people and not only that, fight demonic forces there.

■ Eleven does her best to save Max and stop the villain's reign of terror like she did back in 1979, but Vecna was stronger, transporting El to the far less festive Mind Lair.

HAWKINS

I SURVIVED '85 HAWKINS INDIANA

OMG Gnarly!

WHAT THE HELL IS THE VOID?

When Eleven wants to track someone down she enters a mysterious world called The Void. But what is The Void? And is it even real?

The Void is a psychic realm where Eleven can mentally travel into the space of another being and witness what is going on.

The Void is an endless expanse of black nothing except an ankle-deep ocean to the non-existent horizon. It is empty, lonely and let's face it, creepy as hell.

In some ways we can view The Void as Eleven being alone with her thoughts – her psychic thoughts given a specific direction. In that sense it's only a place that exists in El's imagination. But the things she sees and hears there are very real. Confusing, right?

Henry Creel ominously called The Void, "The Battleground", while Eleven referred to it simply as "The Darkness".

In order to get to The Void, El sometimes needs sensory deprivation.

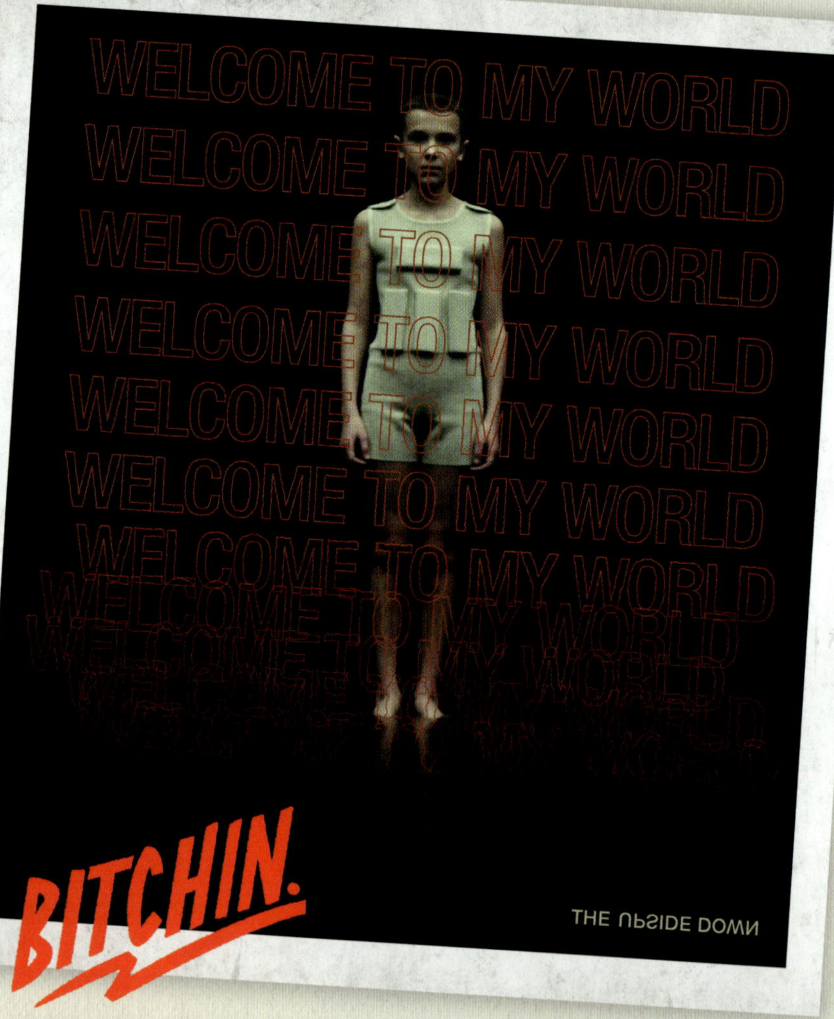

BITCHIN.

■ Sometimes The Void is the loneliest place

At Hawkins National Laboratory they had a massive water tank for Eleven to submerge herself in, dubbed 'The Bath'.

When Eleven mentally jumped to the Upside Down to search for Will, she had to do it in a makeshift bath created from a paddling pool and 1,500 lbs (680 kg) of de-icing salt. The salt was necessary to make her float.

One of the first times El took a psychic walk into The Void, she was sent to spy on a Russian agent. She didn't speak Russian and couldn't understand a word, but The Lab had equipment set up so that they could hear – and translate – what Eleven heard.

■ To enter The Void you need extreme focus

El abandoned that first Void-walk when she heard the growling of an unknown creature.

Intrigued by the growling El had heard, Dr Brenner sent her back into The Void to discover what had made the horrible sound. When she found the creature, it was feasting on the corpse of another animal. Eleven tapped it, thinking she was safe, and that actions in The Void didn't have 'real world' consequences; it turns out she was MASSIVELY WRONG.

When Eleven touched the Demogorgon in The Void, she was making contact with a being from another reality. That impossible act ripped a hole in the space between dimensions allowing creatures like the Demogorgon to come and go from our world as they pleased. Oh well, you live and learn.

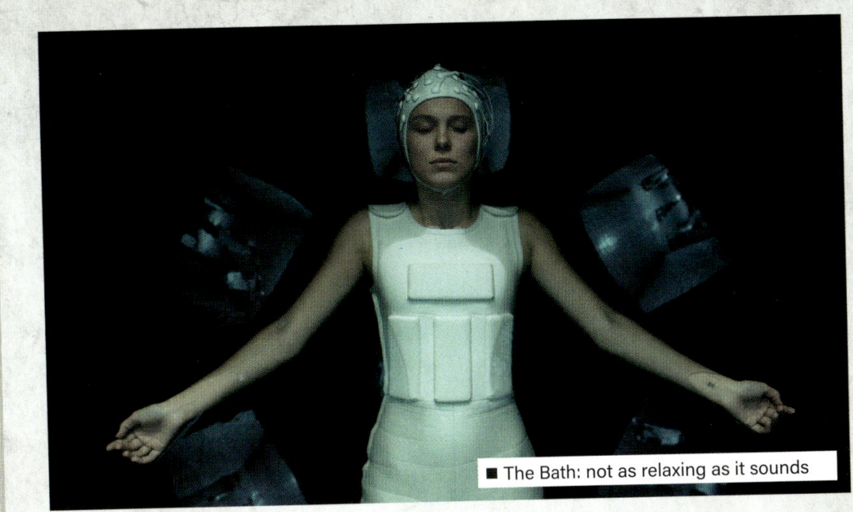
■ The Bath: not as relaxing as it sounds

As Eleven's powers grew she learned how to enter The Void without using the sensory deprivation tank. In 1984, she regularly 'visited' Mike in The Void. Was it spying? Pretty much. Was it ethical? Um, probably not. Did it offer a lifeline to El? Absolutely. Did that make it OK? Er, no.

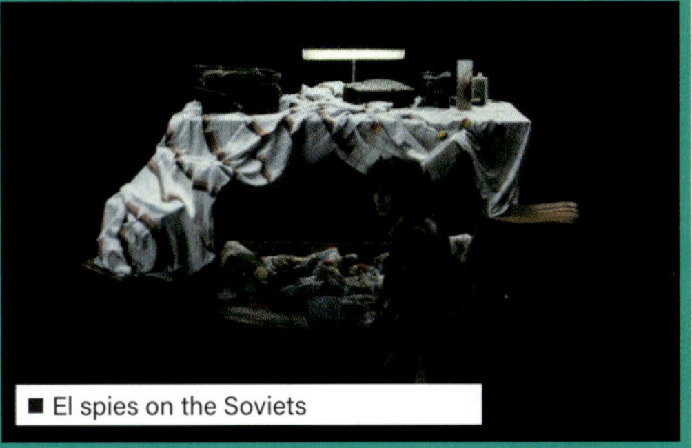
■ El spies on the Soviets

El enters The Void by using a makeshift bandana on her eyes and the sound of static, either from an untuned radio or a television, to block out light and noise.

■ To most of us The Void is something to avoid

■ In The Void you can watch, but you can't help

The Void can also be used to get inside someone's head and 'piggyback' on their memories. Eleven did this with Max in 1986.

Being in The Void is useful for gathering information about what's going on, but it's no substitute for being physically at the scene. When Max was dying, all Eleven could do was watch as Lucas tragically cradled Max's body. That is, until she harnessed a brand new power. By recalling happy memories that they both shared, she appeared to bring Max back to the land of the living. We know that love can overcome evil, but only time will tell if Eleven's gambit paid off.

■ Friends forever?

UPSIDE DOWN SINCE 1983

WHAT TO DO:

It's simple (or is it?), just connect the words to the person who said them.

TRAINING TEST

WHO SAID IT?

DUSTIN

Dustin has gone to Weathertop to test out Cerebro and he's picking up all sorts of signals from all over the place. But can you help him work out which of his friends he's listening to?!

NANCY

MIKE

MAX

LUCAS

EDDIE

WILL

ERICA

JONATHAN

ARGYLE

ELEVEN

A. "RUN!"

B. "WE HAVE A LOT OF RULES IN OUR PARTY, BUT THE MOST IMPORTANT IS, 'FRIENDS DON'T LIE.'"

C. "IF ANYONE ASKS WHERE I AM, I'VE LEFT THE COUNTRY."

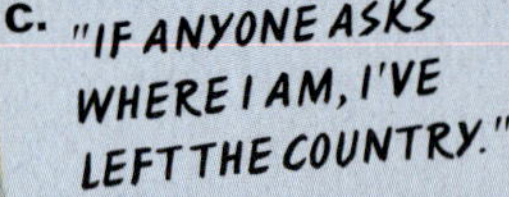

D. "I MADE YOU A NEW MIXTAPE."

E. "WHAT IS, FRIEND?"

F. "AND I LIKE TALKING WITH YOU, STALKER."

G. "WHO WOULD I TELL? YOU'RE MY ONLY FRIEND, JONATHAN."

H. "NOBODY DEVIATES FROM THE PLAN, NO MATTER WHAT."

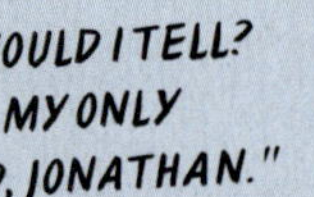

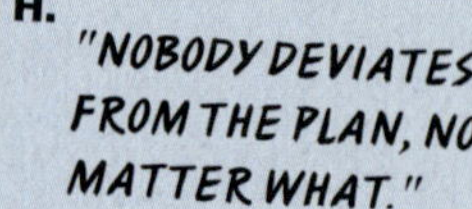

I. "NERD."

J. "CHRISSY, WAKE UP. I DON'T LIKE THIS, CHRISSY. WAKE UP!"

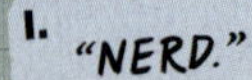

ANSWERS ON PAGE 118

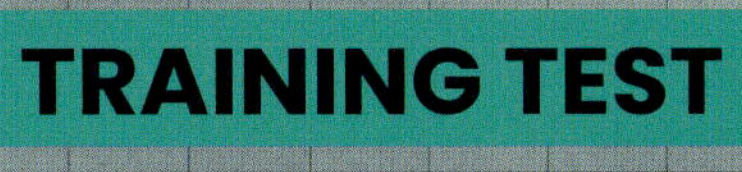

TRAINING TEST

TUNNEL OUT OF THE TUNNEL

Steve Harrington is trapped in the tunnel system under Hawkins and needs you to help him escape before the vines, spores and possibly Dart get him.

WHAT TO DO:

Starting at Merrill's farm, find your way to Steve. Avoid all the deathly dead ends, rescue Steve and weave your way out of the labyrinth and get to the school.

ENTER MERRILL WRIGHT'S PUMPKIN PATCH

HFC

"RESCUE ME!"

EXIT

ANSWERS ON PAGE 119

STRANGER "THINGS"

ARTEFACTS

Some things have an intrinsic power and special relevance. These are the talismans of the troubles in Hawkins.

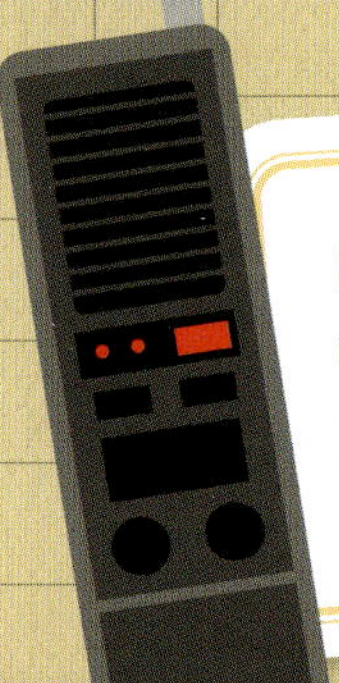

WALKIE TALKIES

How do you communicate with friends who are some distance away? Walkie talkies or pigeons. That's it.

DENS

Castle Byers gave Will a hiding place, and Mike had his basement den where El hid out.

FAIRY LIGHTS

Harnessing the power of light is something humans have been doing forever. Joyce just perfected it.

TIGERS

The Hawkins High School mascot. Ferocious but oh-so-cute.

HAM RADIO

A radio that can transmit over thousands of miles. It is illegal for a civilian to transmit without a license, but anyone can tune in and listen.

SKATEBOARD

Everyone should have a thing, y'know, to stand out. Max's things are a skateboard and a Walkman.

STEVE'S BAT

Steve's bat was actually first used by Jonathan. It's the nails that make it gnarly.

DUSTIN'S CAP

Nothing wrong with a signature look. Especially one that goes with EVERYTHING.

BARB'S GLASSES

How are these so iconic? They just are.

ERICA'S TORCH HAT

In terms of DIY thingamabobs, Erica's torch headgear lights the way.

BINOCULARS

If Lucas doesn't have his binoculars it's probably because he's lent them to Max.

CEREBRO

Cerebro is Dustin's ham radio on Weathertop hill.

CHERRY SLUSHIE

For Yuri, no other frozen fruit drink will do.

D&D GAME

Escaping into a world of monsters and magic is less appealing when you live in a world of monsters and magic.

PIZZA

A pizza with pineapple – that's one of your 5-a-day right there.

GHETTO BLASTER

Perfect for 'blasting' out The Clash and blocking out bad vibes.

EGGOS

They're waffles. They're made by Kellogg's. They're the only thing Eleven seems to eat.

GRANDFATHER CLOCK

Cursed in the Creel House

BANDANAS AND SCARVES

Either on Lucas' forehead or around El's eyes.

ARCADE GAMES

MADMAX destroyed the high scores. Dustin is displeased, Keith isn't bothered.

STRANGER "THINGS"

WEAPONS

Eleven isn't the only weapon in the war on the Upside Down. Pointy stuff comes in pretty handy too.

HATCHET JOB

Joyce Byers was the first Hawkins resident to seriously weapon up. She went to the shed, got an axe, took a spot on the sofa and prepared to fight the Demogorgon – singlehandedly – if it showed up in her lounge.

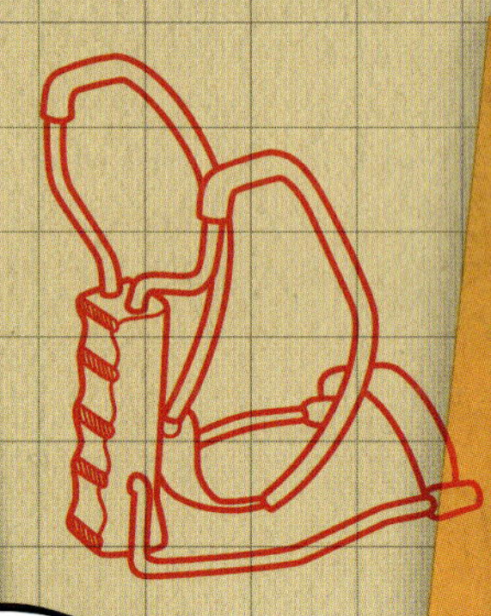

LUCAS IS READY FOR IT

At the first sign of trouble Lucas had his kitbag packed. For 'Operation Mirkwood' he was all set: "Binoculars ... from 'Nam. Army knife ... also from 'Nam. Hammer, camouflage bandana, and the wrist rocket." The wrist rocket is a slingshot – which might not seem very badass, but Lucas actually used it to distract the Demogorgon in the Starcourt Mall giving his gang a chance to get away.

Defend yourself DIY style

FOR COMMUNICATION & NUTRITION

FOR CONCENTRATION

DISTRACT IT!

DEMOGORGAN HUNTING

STARTER KIT

FOR PROTECTION

SEE IT!

LURE IT!

BASH IT!

YOU CAN'T RUN BEFORE YOU WALK(IE TALKIE)

No campaign can work without a leader giving directions or sending you early warning signals, which is why Mike chose the walkie talkie. He's the most effective communicator of the group, unless he's talking to girls, then it's game over, over.

NOTHING FANCY FOR NANCY

Nancy chose the easily-wielded, streamlined baseball bat as her weapon of choice for her Demogorgon hunting spree. In her tight grip, the slender but powerful bat becomes an extension of her arm, giving the long-limbed, no-faced monster from another world a run for its gangly money.

HARRINGTON NAILS IT

What's a better weapon than a baseball bat? A baseball bat with a bunch of nails sticking out of it! Steve knows how to make a thing (himself) into a better thing (good hair), so naturally he evolved the humble baseball bat into a clobbering whacker that would do serious damage to anything that got in its path. Also useful for picking up discarded Demodog skin without getting slimy fingers.

EDDIE'S BIN THERE

When the lord of the underworld starts a fight, you don't always have time to go to the shops, which is why Eddie fashioned himself a spear and a shield from a dustbin lid with a smattering of nails for good measure. Sadly, it wasn't enough. Rock on, Eddie Munson.

DEMO BATS

ASSAULT ON VECNA

Fighting alt-world scary monsters is hard, but ending the daddy of the Upside Down, that requires more firepower. By the time the brave kids of Hawkins High School met the ultimate foe they went in swinging: Steve with a massive axe and Nancy, queen of all artillery, with a shotgun! As an actual victim of Vecna, not to mention Barb's best friend, she had a personal score to settle.

DO NOT MESS WITH THIS LITTLE SISTER

When Erica joined the Scoops Troop in 1985, she was dubious about the potential "child endangerment" she was getting into. A year later, she was casually fashioning weapons and fixing knives onto the end poles. A girl with a sharp tongue and a spear to match – now that's something to run from.

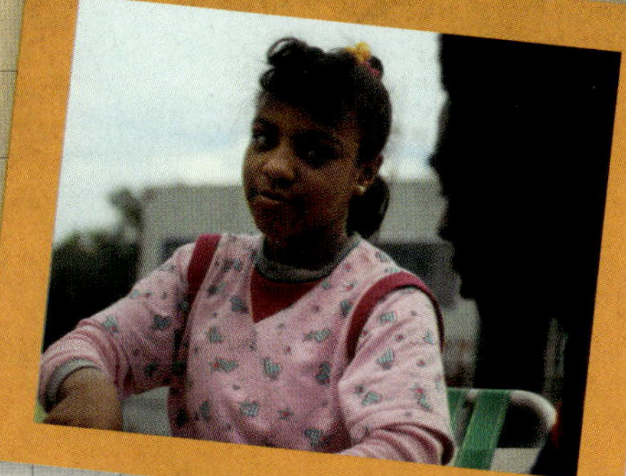

CLUB TOGETHER

Jonathan had a golf club, but then he ditched it: silly man. Hold onto your weapons. You never know when a portal will open up and pull you into dark inescapable hell.

STRANGER "THINGS"

VEHICLES

Want to spot friends and foes at a distance? You need to know what wheels they're rolling in on.

SAFE

STEVE'S BMW

This is the vehicle you want to ride shotgun in. The Germans know how to make a reliable automobile and Steve Harrington knows how to drive, priding himself on his babysitter skills and deliverer of children to their destinations. Steve's 733i Bimmer is like the school bus, but cooler, faster and with a much sicker radio.

SAFE

SURFER BOY PIZZA VAN

Argyle is not necessarily the sort of person you would peg as a 'responsible driver,' but he wouldn't intentionally try to kill you, and in this current climate, that's a win. Plus, he might have a tasty pizza pie steaming on the backseat, so, if you do crash at least you'll do it on a full stomach.

RISKY

MAX'S SKATEBOARD

If Max is on the skateboard coming to your rescue, that's fantastic news. If her skateboard is your only means of escape, not so good. Hope you have some knee pads.

DANGER

BILLY'S CAMARO

Even before the Mind Flayer flayed Billy's brain he was a troubled character and not someone you'd want to catch a lift from. When he became possessed he was even less appealing.

DANGER

EDDIE'S TRAILER

Eddie is stand-up guy – give or take a few minor felonies – and his trailer should be a safe space. Sadly, Vecna marked Chrissy as a victim when she was visiting the house on wheels, and it became a gateway to the Upside Down and therefore not a place you should hang out.

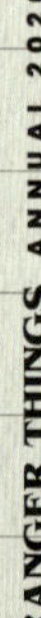

RISKY

YURI'S PLANE

The likelihood of finding yourself at Yuri's Fish N' Fly in deepest Alaska is slim, but if you happen to be on a skiing holiday and fancy a day trip to Russia, do not accept a ride with Comrade Yuri Ismaylov in his Antonov An-2 aircraft. Intel on his mental-wellbeing is inconclusive, and the service-record of his clapped out banger of an aircraft, one which has recently been in a crash, is poor.

HAWKINS POWER AND LIGHT VAN

If you've got a problem with power outages or are worried about overloading plug sockets, do not call these people. They are no good. They do not care about getting your VCR and Atari to run efficiently, they want to do experiments on you and your children and hush up their slimy gateway to a multiverse of horror. Bad people: not cool.

BICYCLES

Kids on bikes are cool. Max and Dustin can often be spotted on BMX's, while Mike has a Schwinn that his friend El liked to hop on the back of. Hawkins is a small town and a lot of kids get about on two wheels, most are harmless, but some might be Hawkins Tigers basketball players with a grudge. If you see one of those, it's time to pedal.

GOVERNMENT HELICOPTERS

The US government have a lot of concerns, your safety is not one of them. Choppers must be stopped, by any means necessary.

RISKY

POLICE VEHICLES

If you hear the siren and see the flashing blue and red lights, ask yourself this question: is it Hop or is it not? Hawkins Police Department are here to help, but they are not always the brightest sparks and might slow you down. Chief Hopper is a king among men, Officer Callahan and Officer Powell are fairly well-meaning, but avoid State Troopers! You can trust these out-of-towners about as far as you can throw a fake corpse.

STRANGER LOOKS

FASHION

Looking good is important, especially when it might be your last day on earth. Here's some tips on dressing for the monster annihilation.

NO SLEEVES, NO PROBLEM

You know you're in Hawkins when everyone has removed the sleeves from something and slipped it over the top of something else. It's a chilly town and so layering makes sense, plus it gives you easy mobility. The good guys do it, the bad guys, the kids, the mums, everyone's at it!

UNIFORMS

Wearing the same thing every day is a drag, but it means you have more time to worry about the important things, like what socks and pants to wear.

CLIQUES ARE NOT CHIC

Dressing to signal your affiliation with one group or another is cool for the other members, but it can alienate those who can't dunk from the 3-point line, or shred Mötley Crüe. In that instance you need to find common ground, even if it's underground.

COLOURPHOBIA IS NOT CUTE

Newsflash! People who are scared of colour are scary. If you think wearing yellow and pink and turquoise and blue and red at the same time is unserious, then maybe *you're* the monster.

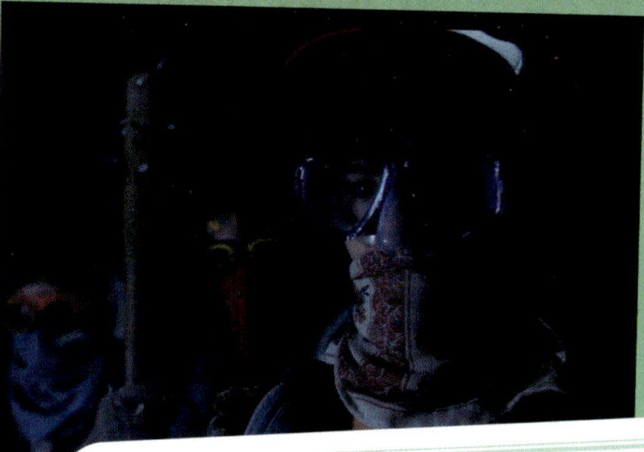

PROTECT YOURSELF

Going into battle in a tunnel? The very least you can do is cover your nose, mouth and eyes. Swimming goggles and diving masks (paired with your mum's favourite tea towel) should do the trick for a twenty-minute campaign. Longer trips will require more substantial body armour, weapons and military-grade headgear.

EXPRESS YOURSELF

Wear what you're comfortable in and what screams 'wear me' from your wardrobe. It doesn't matter how massively baggy it is, or how much your dress clashes with your shirt, you do you. Borrowing someone else's vibe is fine too. Mike's crazy visor shows Argyle that the little dude has been taking style notes.

MAKE AN EFFORT

It doesn't matter how lazy you are, or how bad your day is, you should always make an effort with your appearance, it shows other people - and undead monsters - you mean business.

DRESSING WITH A MESSAGE

When you really love something, you want to surround yourself with that thing. When Dustin went to Camp Know Where, he met his first girlfriend Suzie. It was such a special time that after he'd been there and done that, he literally bought the T-shirt and also the baseball cap. Now those happy memories are with him wherever he goes – unless it's wash day.

ACCESSORIZE

Accessories are a simple way to set yourself apart from the crowd and they don't have to set you back a bomb. A simple pair of glasses made from an old pizza box look fly and they block out 100% of the sun's harmful UVA and UVB rays.

HATS: NOT FOR EVERYONE

Some of us suit a hat. Vickie looks adorable in a straw boater. Dustin suits a hat. Without a baseball cap he looks weird at this point. But Will's awesome bowl cut just doesn't work with a magician's pointy cap. It's flimsy, cumbersome, and frankly the only person to slay that look was Mickey Mouse.

A bitchin' headband not only soaks up the sweat of fear when you're fighting for your life, but it also keeps the hair out of your eyes and makes you look like Rambo. OG headband boy Lucas started this trend, FYI.

A-Z OF STUFF YOU NEED TO KNOW

This essential encyclopedia contains just a fraction of the information connected to the horrific happenings in Hawkins ...

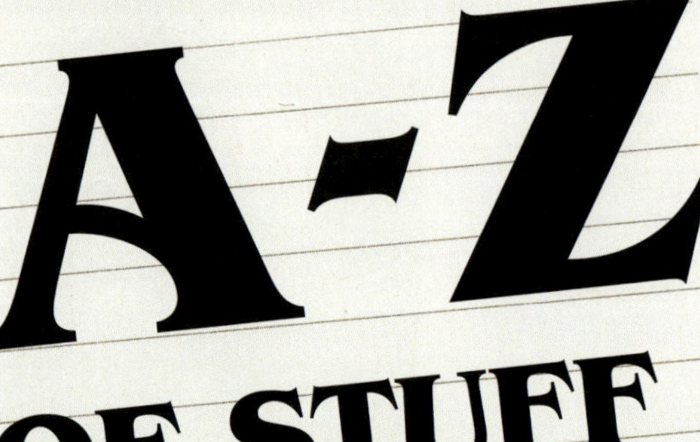

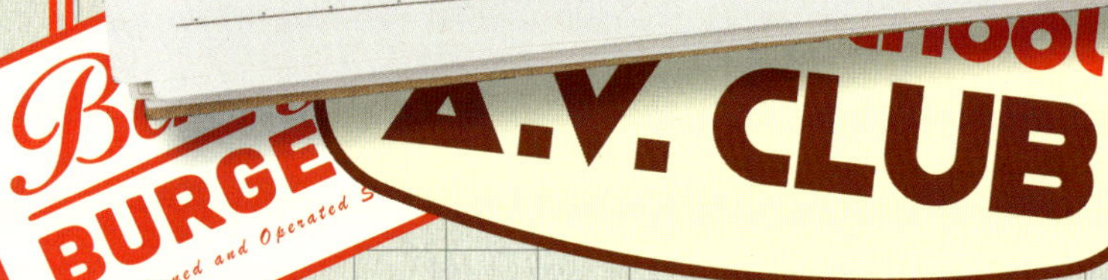

A | AV CLUB
Audio/Visual Club at Hawkins Middle School – members included Will, Mike, Lucas and Dustin.

B | BENNY'S BURGERS
Diner where El escapes to, and the Hawkins Tigers basketball team's hangout.

C | CORRODED COFFIN
Eddie's totally gnarly metal band, other members include: Gareth, Jeff and Freak 1.

D | DEPARTMENT OF ENERGY
The cover-name for the unethical operation taking place at the Hawkins National Laboratory.

E | ENZO
Cryptic sign-off used in the letter to Joyce from Russian guard Dmitri to let her know it was actually from Hopper. (They were supposed to have a date at Enzo's restaurant).

F | FAKE WILL BYERS
Hawkins Lab created a fake body of Will Byers, to hide the fact he was snatched by the Demogorgon.

H | HAWKINS TUNNELS
A series of interconnected tunnels to and from the Upside Down, running under Hawkins.

I | INDIGO
The name given to the experimental program at HNL that involved child subjects, including Eleven.

J | JUNKYARD
Top Hawkins hide-out spot – especially the abandoned bus.

K | KYRZRAN
Village in Kamchatka where comrade Yuri owns a church.

L | LENORA HILLS
Town where Jane Hopper (aka Eleven) and the Byers relocated.

M | MIRKWOOD
The nickname given to the road (after the forest in JRR Tolkein's The Hobbit), where Will was abducted by the Demogorgon.

N | NINA PROJECT
Experiments run by former Hawkins National Laboratory employees in the Nevada desert to get Eleven to relive her past.

O | OZEROV
Russian Army Colonel, stationed at Starcourt Base, who interrogated Steve and Robin.

P | PENHURST MENTAL HOSPITAL
The facility where Victor Creel was committed after supposedly offing his family.

Q | QUARRY
Location where the fake Will Byers' body was dumped.

R | RADIOACTIVE CANISTERS
The power-source used for opening the gate to the Upside Down.

S | SOTERIA
Tiny implant that inhibits Hawkins Lab patients' psychokinetic ability – 011 removed it from 001's neck.

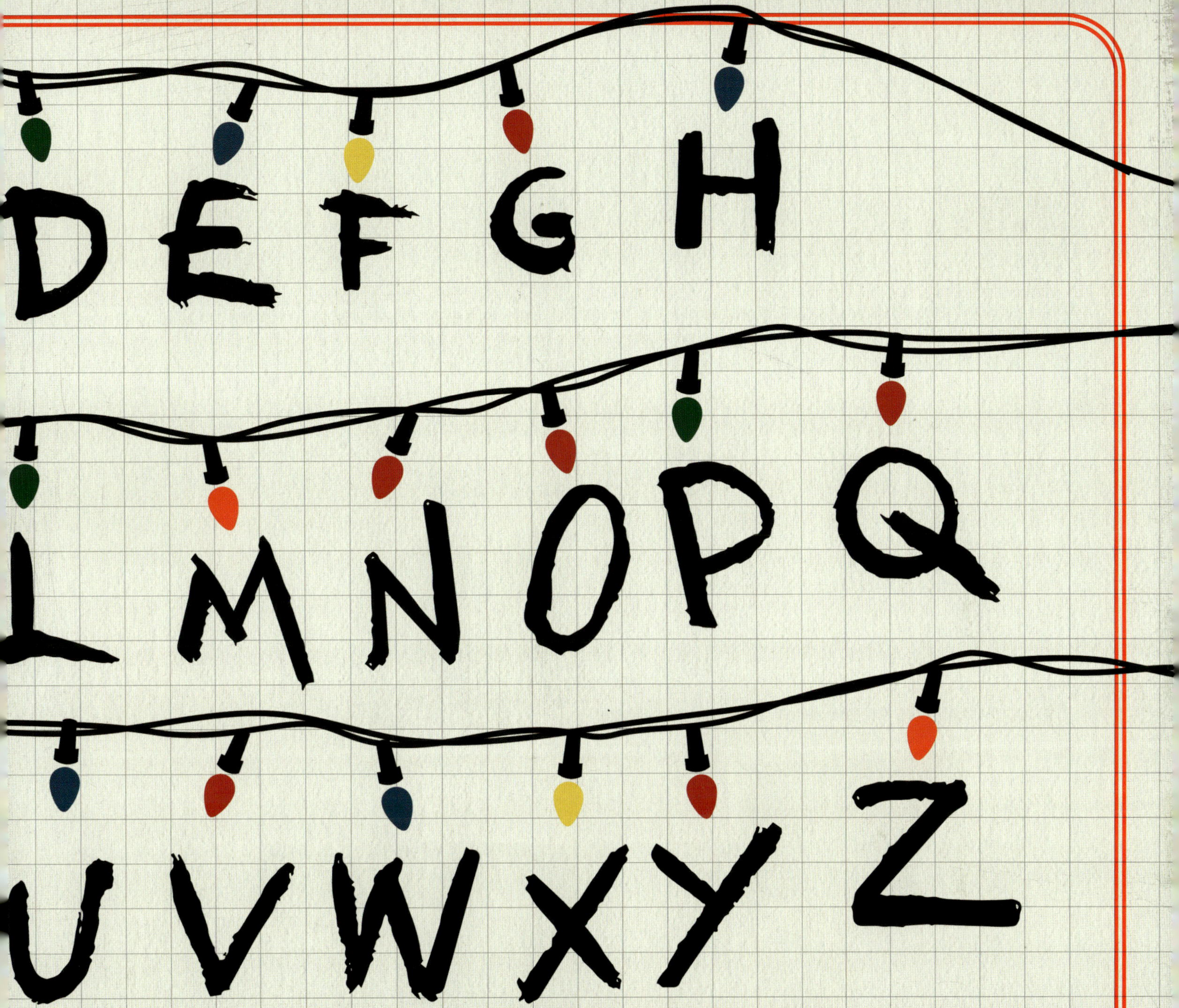

T | TODFTHR
The licence plate on a 1984 Cadillac Eldorado used by Jim Hopper to transfer Dr Alexei to Hawkins.

U | UPSIDE DOWN EGGS
Enormous eggs exist in the Upside Down, but what hatches out of them is unknown ...

V | VINES
Lifeform from the Upside Down, a seemingly sentient plant.

W | WEATHERTOP
(Another Tolkein reference, this time Lord of the Rings). The highest point in Hawkins, a hill where Dustin used radio device, 'Cerebro' to contact Suzie.

X | XMAS LIGHTS
Joyce Byers' festive method of communication with Will in the Upside Down.

Y | YURI'S FISH N' FLY
Alaskan/Russian cover-business for a smuggling operation that seems to be peanut butter focused.

Z | ZERO
Was there a patient zero before 001's, Henry Creel?

TRAINING TEST

POP QUIZ

The heroes of Hawkins are massive geeks, even Erica! Are you nerdy enough to know the pop culture references that fill their lives?

1. **When Robin gets a job at Family Video she says that her favourite films are The Apartment, Children of Paradise and The Hidden Fortress. What do these movies have in common?**

A. They all star Shirley MacLaine
B. They are all foreign films
C. They are all black and white
D. They are all cartoons

2. **What's the missing name in this sentence spoken by Jonathan to Will?**
"Who would you rather be friends with? ________ or Kenny Rogers?"

A. Billy
B. Budgie
C. Blondie
D. Bowie

3. **Which Dungeons & Dragons monster have 'The Party' not yet mentioned?**

A. Mind Flayer
B. Thessalhydra
C. Demogorgon
D. Tarrasque

4. **Which of the Ghostbusters did Lucas not want to be?**

A. Ray Stantz
B. Egon Spengler
C. Winston Zedlemore
D. Peter Venkman

5. **Which popular slang word means bad (not good)?**

A. Tubular
B. Bitchin'
C. Gnarly
D. Grody

6. **The name Mirkwood, the name given to a road in Hawkins, is inspired by which fantasy book?**

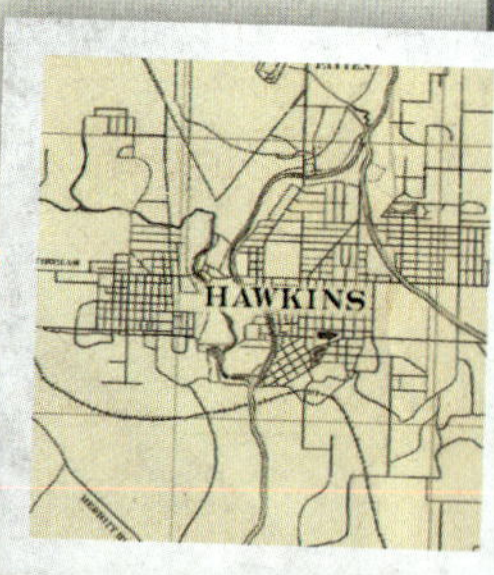

A. The Hobbit
B. The Hulk
C. The Stand
D. The Rats

7. **Who is Nancy's celebrity crush?**

A. Michael J. Fox
B. Tom Cruise
C. Ralph Macchio
D. Bruce Willis

8. **Dustin Compares Eleven to one of The X-Men, which one?**

A. Rogue
B. Jean Grey
C. Professor X
D. Beast

9. **Mike, Will, Lucas and Dustin snuck into a screening of which dead scary film?**

A. Day of the Dead
B. The Evil Dead
C. Dawn of the Dead
D. Night of the Living Dead

10.

Suzie is a fan of a film and is reading a book about what same subject?

A. Witches (The Witches and Escape From Witch Mountain)

B. Castles (Howl's Moving Castle and Castle in The Sky)

C. Princesses (The Princess Bride and Sleeping Beauty)

D. Wizards (The Wizard of Earthsea and The Wizard of Oz)

11.

Which one of these posters is NOT hanging on Mike, Nancy or Jonathan's bedroom walls?

A. The Dark Crystal

B. Blondie

C. Evil Dead

D. Karate Kid

12.

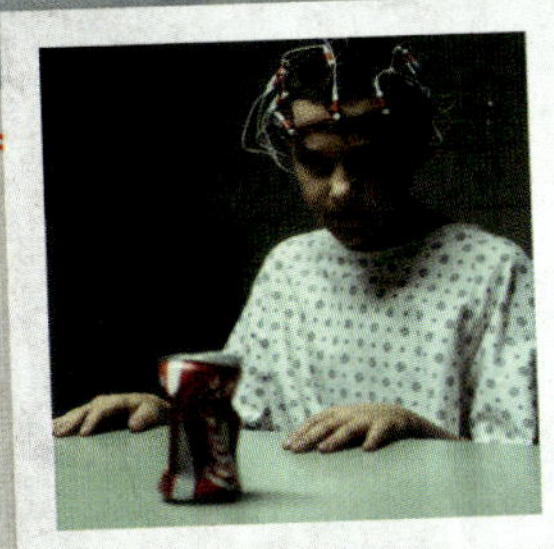

Which two people are a fan of 'New' Coke, a beverage introduced in 1985?

A. Erica and Robin

B. Lucas and Mrs Wheeler

C. Mike and Eleven

D. Steve and Officer Callahan

13.

Dustin nicknamed Robin and Steve after which fictional pairing?

A. Heckle and Jeckle

B. Tweedledum and Tweedledee

C. Bert & Ernie

D. Scooby and Shaggy

14.

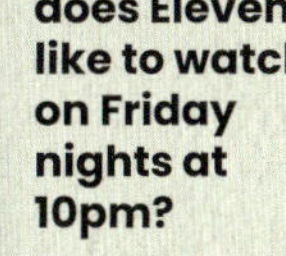

Erica's D&D name Lady Applejack is inspired by what children's toy/cartoon?

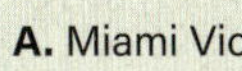

A. Jem and The Holograms

B. The Care Bears

C. My Little Pony

D. Polly Pocket

15.

What show does Eleven like to watch on Friday nights at 10pm?

A. Miami Vice

B. Knight Rider

C. Moonlighting

D. Dallas

16.

When Dustin says, "Never tell me the odds." Who is he quoting?

A. Rick Deckard

B. Indiana Jones

C. Han Solo

D. Jack Ryan

17.

Eddie Munson wears a mask of Michael Myers, who is a character in which horror franchise?

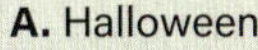

A. Halloween

B. Poltergeist

C. Hellraiser

D. Amityville

18.

When Eleven arrives at the Nina Project, she is so infamous to the staff there that Dr Owens compares her to which pop star?

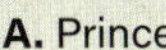

A. Prince

B. Cher

C. Sting

D. Madonna

19.

The Nina Project is named after ...

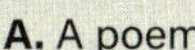

A. A poem

B. A painting

C. An opera

D. A statue

20.

Max's favourite song is Running Up That Hill by Kate Bush. What album is it on?

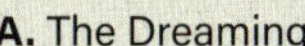

A. The Dreaming

B. Hounds of Love

C. Lionheart

D. Never Forever

ANSWERS ON PAGE 119

WHAT WENT DOWN IN '85

Shopping, a Russian takeover, zombies who eat soil: welcome to a new dawn of the 'dead weird'.

Friends don't Lie

■ Eleven and Mike have gotten close, really close and Hopper hates it. Hop tells Mike to leave El alone or never see her again. Mike does what he's told, making excuses and lying. New bestie, Max, encourages El to "dump his ass," which she does at the brand new Starcourt Mall.

■ Everyone at Hawkins Community Pool had the hots for Billy who had a job as a lifeguard there, but in a weird turn of events, Billy ended up sweating his mullet off, it was literally 'too hot.' Billy had been 'possessed' by the Mind Flayer, an Upside Down entity, who likes it cold, and wanted to build an army of braindead residents, The Flayed. The Mind Flayer, who had been mere smoke when he took over Will's mind, decided to upgrade himself with a fleshy avatar to physically carry out his horrible crimes. The Spider Monster made up of deconstructed rats and melted people was totally rank and frankly terrifying.

■ Starcourt Mall was a cover operation for the Russian government who wanted to open a portal to the Upside Down with a special machine called 'The Key,' so they could use the creatures that live there for no good.

■ Steve got a job at an ice cream shop inside the mall with a girl from school called Robin. Dustin told them that he'd intercepted a Russian message and they started to investigate, somehow ending up deep in the bowels of the mall.

■ Hopper and Joyce were looking into a strange number of abandoned properties, when they discovered Russian agents in the basement of the Hess Farmhouse and take one of them - Alexei - hostage, hoping to discover what the heck is happening. It doesn't end well.

Robin

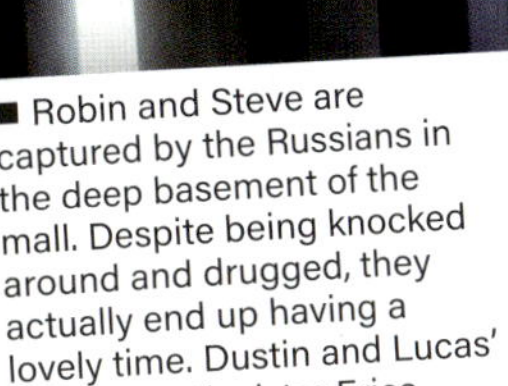

■ Robin and Steve are captured by the Russians in the deep basement of the mall. Despite being knocked around and drugged, they actually end up having a lovely time. Dustin and Lucas' smart-mouth sister Erica helps them escape.

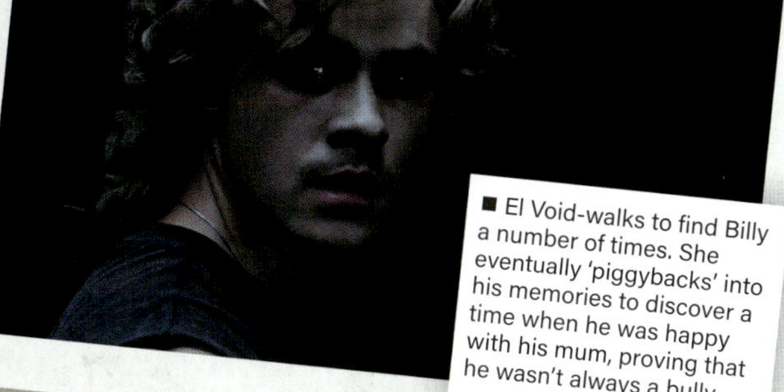

■ El Void-walks to find Billy a number of times. She eventually 'piggybacks' into his memories to discover a time when he was happy with his mum, proving that he wasn't always a bully.

■ El discovers that The Flayed and the Spider Monster are hiding out at Brimborn Steelworks on Cherry Oak Drive.

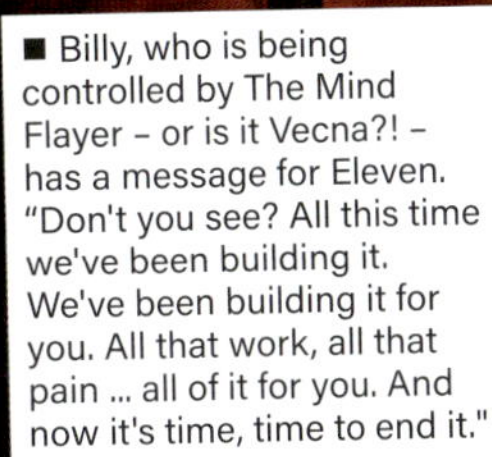

■ Billy, who is being controlled by The Mind Flayer – or is it Vecna?! – has a message for Eleven. "Don't you see? All this time we've been building it. We've been building it for you. All that work, all that pain ... all of it for you. And now it's time, time to end it."

Then he tells her that he's going to kill her and all of her friends. Not cool.

■ The gang race to the mall for a final showdown with the meat-puppet Spider Monster thingy: The Battle of Starcourt. Eleven has lost her powers. She's not able to kill it. The gang chuck fireworks at the slobbering beast but it's not enough.

■ Just when it looks like the monster will kill a defenceless Eleven, Billy steps up and saves her. He sacrifices himself and dies a hero.

■ Meanwhile Joyce and Hopper destroy 'The Key' in the basement and close the gate to The Upside Down.

BAD IDEA!

No matter how thirsty you were, drinking the neon green radioactive fuel would've been the worst idea ever – Erica!

RAD IDEA!

Nancy ignoring her lame-o sexist bosses and following her instincts as a journalist to uncover an unbelievable, but real story.

YOU RULE | YOU SUCK

CLOSE UP ON...

SCOOPS AHOY

AHOY

They don't just sell ice cream at Scoops Ahoy, they investigate international plots to import other-worldly creatures.

Hey, Dingus, your children are here.

■ Band dweeb Robin Buckley is the sassy Scoops Ahoy server poised to give you a moreish dollop of lols with your frozen dairy desert.

YOU SUCK!

You suck

■ When Steve was forced by his dad to get a job at Scoops Ahoy, everyone assumed that the dashing dude would draw all the girls to the parlour, but somehow they don't fall for his cheesy patter and his attention turns to his kooky colleague Robin.

"This stupid hat. It's blowing my best feature."

Steve

The place to be

■ The Starcourt Mall was an instant hit with the local kids. A stop off at Scoops Ahoy was pretty much obligatory.

The customer is always right

■ The best/worst customer at Scoops Ahoy was Erica Sinclair, an ice cream fiend who was never-not lurking, testing patience and demanding samples of every flavour.

НЕДЕЛЯ ДЛИННАЯ
The week is long
СЕРЕБРЯНЫЙ КОТ ЕСТ
the silver cat feeds
КОГДА СИНЕЕ ВСТРЕТИТСЯ
when blue meets
С ЖЁЛТЫМ НА ЗАПАДЕ
yellow in the west

Dusty Bun and Suzie Poo

■ Dustin intercepted a secret Russian communication on Cerebro, his special ham radio designed to chat with new long-distance girlfriend, Suzie. Language-whizz Robin, who speaks Spanish and French, Italian and fluent Pig Latin took it upon herself to translate Dustin's secret message. But when she did, it didn't make much sense.

Mystery boxes

■ After Robin, Dustin and Steve work out that the secret message is about a hush-hush drop-off, they see Russians loading boxes into a storage room. They decide they need to know what's in the boxes.

■ "Commence operation child endangerment."

What's in it for Erica?

■ The only problem is that the air vent leading to the storage room is too small. They bribe perma-customer Erica with the offer of a lifetime supply of ice cream and she agrees to it.

It looks suss to me

■ The Scoops Troop discovers that the boxes are packed with a gnarly-looking green liquid that melts anything it touches.

Dream team

■ Scoops Troop investigate the Russian invasion. Get trapped. Captured. Beat up. Share stories. Bond. Escape.

Mission complete

■ All Scoops Troop members made it out of the mall alive ready to fight another day – or rather ...

... work another day at the Video store.

■ The continuing adventures of Tweedledee and Tweedledum.

FLAVOURS OF THE DAY

U.S.S. Butterscotch
Peanut Butter Chocolate Swirl
Cherries Jubilee
Peppermint stick

MAKEOVER OR DISGUISE?

Everyone loves a makeover, especially if it allows you to pass unnoticed past the bad men.

■ Which Quality Street are you dressing up as?

■ Say, 'yellow' to summer style!

MALLRAT MATERIAL GIRLS

When Max and El hit the Starcourt Mall for a makeover it was 1985! That's peak 80s! The best 80s! There was no way they wouldn't look incredible when they hit the racks of JC Penney. El's first purchase was a brightly coloured playsuit romper that was giving Matisse cut outs and beach towel vibes.

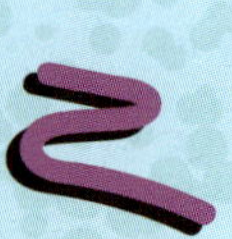

CHEAP FRILLS!

When you want people to take you seriously, you might consider dressing like a little dolly or your grandma going to a wedding. 'Rose' and 'Ruth' were very uncomfortable in their polyester blouses and drip-dry two-piece suits, but despite the rashes they looked sensational. Sure, Robin thinks she looks ridiculous. But frilly things can confuse and confound, especially if you stand up, shout and wave your hands a lot.

GETTING WIGGY WITH IT!

For some reason, little girls don't have shaved heads very often, so when Eleven wanted to walk around Hawkins without being noticed, Mike found her a blonde wig to wear. The pink party dress, designed for a toddler's tea party, finished off the look that said more about how boys think girls dress rather than how they actually look. Did El blend in? Not really. Stealing boxes and boxes of Eggos and smashing store windows would draw attention to anyone, no matter what they were wearing, tbh.

GIRL BOSS GOTH

Jane Ives might turn out to be the most powerful woman in the world. During a brief trip to Chicago, Eleven experimented with a look that showcased all of that girl boss power: black blazer with massive shoulder pads, crisp gelled hair and masses of skunk-liner. With this bold makeover she looked like she could crush any man like a Coke can – which she absolutely could.

TRAINING TEST

MATCHY MATCHY

Find the two pictures of Max and Eleven that match exactly. There are only two.

ANSWERS ON PAGE 119

FRIENDS

You can never have too many friends, especially if they're like this plucky bunch ...

The good guys are all friends in Hawkins, but some of these buddies are closer than others. Maybe it's because circumstances pushed them together, maybe it's because they've been through a lot that no one else can understand, or maybe they just dig their vibe and lusciously shiny hair. Whatever the reason, the support these guys give each other is a super-power that just about matches Eleven's.

■ Friends don't lie: they hug

FRIENDS DON'T LIE

Robin and Steve

■ When Steve started working at Scoops Ahoy and began to get to know Robin, he liked everything about her and developed a bit of a crush. Their chemistry is incredible, but when Robin revealed she wasn't into him like that, he didn't take it badly, he moved on, showing how much he's grown since he ditched his loser friends Carol and Tommy. Now he has a platonic soulmate who'll stick with him through thick and thin, not someone who would make him feel small and dump him on any given Tuesday.

El and Max

■ Max and Eleven didn't hit it off straight away, on account of El thinking Max was coming after her boyfriend, but as soon as that misunderstanding was sorted, the two bonded and became besties, shopping, gossiping and trying to shut out the harsh realties of life – at least until they've picked a bitchin' outfit. The two female members of The Party had fun trash-talking the boys and even spying on them, but when the time came to get serious, the playing stopped and the fighting side-by-side to the bitter end started.

Will and Mike

■ Most of us can only dream of a lifelong friendship like Will and Mike have. Sure, all four members of the OG Party are close, but Mike and Will have been friends forever. In 1983, Mike took Will's disappearance the hardest, and when Will felt that Mike was replacing him with Eleven it's safe to say he was pretty devo-ed. But friendship is a long, twisty journey and they will always be there for each other – won't they?

Nancy and Robin

■ The most unlikely friendship of all is between Nancy, the popular good girl, and Robin, the school band dweeb. Why does it work? Because those labels are utter nonsense. Nancy is actually a badass and so is Robin. The pair teamed up to track down Victor Creel, the father of Vecna himself, but their partnership was much more than just workmates. After the death of her best friend Barb, no-nonsense Nancy really needed a friend, especially with Jonathan miles away in Cali, so when eccentric Robin breezed into her life, she couldn't have arrived at a better time. Each pushes the other to be better, to be more confident and to do whatever's necessary to get the darn thing done.

Steve and Eddie

■ Of course, Dustin and Eddie got on like a house on fire, but Eddie and Steve – aka Steddie – was the friendship neither guy expected. One was a freakazoid metal-head from a trailer park, the other was a douchey prom king wannabe with a BMW. But being a genuinely decent person cuts through the noise of who has what to who does what. And both were pretty heroic. Dustin looked up to Steve, but Eddie gave Steve someone to look up to, and well, Eddie was surprised at how pretty boy Steve was actually pretty metal and started to admire him back. Put it down to the influence of the Upside Down or maybe the power of the sleeveless denim jacket.

Dustin and Steve

■ When Dustin needed help with Dart no one was around, except Steve 'the hair' Harrington. Dustin's a smart cookie, so he knew that some help was better than none and the two teamed up. From that day onwards, the unlikely pairing have gone from strength to strength. From babysitter, to brothers in arms to the bromance of the 20th century. Now Steve needs Dustin, like he needs four spritzes of hairspray, and Dustin thinks Steve is "awesome".

Lucas and Dustin

■ The original wisecracking twosome is Lucas and Dustin. Dustin is such a smart alec and Lucas is so pure-hearted that together they're a pretty neat team. When Will was snatched by the Demogorgon and Mike started to hang out with Eleven, of course Dustin and Lucas spent more time together. The way they confide in each other, sleep on each others' shoulders, tease each other without being mean and don't let a girl (Max) come between them is gold-star behaviour. Lucas goes the extra mile for Dustin, like when he literally climbs into a dumpster to find Dart. Dustin meanwhile, is a literal friend-machine – even forming an unbreakable bond with Lucas' kid sister Erica. One geek can spot another, right?

HOW TO DEFEAT THE DARKNESS

JOKES

Hawkins is a scary town, but it's also filled with a lot of very funny people, here are some of their best moments.

There's a saying that 'you have to laugh or else you'd cry', and that pretty much sums up a lot of the antics in Hawkins. The residents have to get up and face the day, which may or may not contain a monster with a bad attitude. You have to laugh. Luckily the people of Hawkins are able to laugh a lot because those fools are funny. But who's the biggest joker?

Dude.

ROBIN

"HOW MANY CHILDREN ARE YOU FRIENDS WITH?"

Answer: All of them.

"CAN YOU REDIRECT YOUR STREAM PLEASE."

When you gotta go, you gotta go.

"IN THE MEANTIME, SLING ICE CREAM, BEHAVE AND DON'T GET BEAT UP."

The mother of Scoops has spoken.

ARGYLE

"TRY BEFORE YOU DENY BROCHACHOS."

Go on, give it a go!

"OH MY GOD, WHY IS THAT GUY HOLDING A GUN?"

These are important questions!!!

"SINCE WHEN DID WE DECIDE NINA WAS A PHYSICAL BUILDING AND NOT A SMALL WOMAN?"

So many important questions.

MURRAY

"MY FINGERS ARE LIKE ARROWS, MY ARMS LIKE IRON, MY FEET LIKE SPEARS."

Welcome to Delusion, population: Murray Bauman.

"AND IF YOU NEED TO REACH ME AGAIN ... DON'T!"

Thanks so much Mr Helpful.

"WHY IS THIS FOUR-YEAR-OLD SPEAKING TO ME?"

Is the last thing you should say to Erica Sinclair.

YURI

"HE LOVE BEARS. THEY BROKE HIS HEART. OR RATHER PUNCTURED IT WITH THEIR BEAR CLAWS."

Bears are cute but ferocious.

"I LOVE THE SMELL OF CASH IN MORNING."

Fresh coffee's nice too.

"GET YOUR HANDS OFF ME, POTATOHEAD."

Is not a Toy Story quote.

ERICA

"PLEASE DON'T CRY NERDS."

Tbh, they can't help themselves.

"EVEN THOUGH YOU'RE A BENCH-RIDING LOSER, YOU'RE STILL MY BROTHER."

Comforting words for Lucas, there.

"JUST THE FACTS."

You can say anything to anyone, as long as you add this three-word phrase to the end.

DUSTIN

"WE NEVER WOULD'VE UPSET YOU IF WE KNEW YOU HAD SUPER POWERS."

Never annoy people who can kill you with their mind.

"TOUCH MY BUTT. I DON'T CARE."

Is something you only say if trapped in an air vent.

"WHY ARE YOU KEEPING THIS CURIOSITY DOOR LOCKED?"

Hey kids! Learning is fun.

STEVE

"C'MON MAN, NOT MY SCOOPER."

Never lick another person's scooper.

"YOU THINK I JUST WEAR THIS? THINK I'M A SPY IN A SAILOR'S UNIFORM?"

... Is exactly what a spy would say.

"SCREW TODD. STEVE'S YOUR DADDY NOW."

RIP Toddfather, hello Stevaddy.

THE WINNER IS ...

Dustin and Steve and Robin and Erica

The Spider Monster of joking around! Smooshed together they're one big scoop of funny.

HOW TO DEFEAT THE DARKNESS

TUNES

In case of interdimensional apocalypse, play this!

Should I Stay or Should I Go, The Clash (1982)

■ How do you communicate with your mum when a monster captures you and takes you to an alternate reality? You play your favourite song over and over and hope that it drifts between the worlds. The song you love, that your big brother introduced to you means something. Softly singing the song to himself gave Will strength to stay alive, it grounded him and connected him to his family. While he sang the song, Will was making up his mind to survive or give up. He chose to fight, and survive. Very punk!

Never Ending Story, Limahl (1984)

■ Suzie Poo and Dusty Bun proved that an utterly cringe sing-a-long can work as a transcendent moment to fire up the troops! Their belting long-distance performance was so pure that only good could come from it. After that over-share of silly, sappy, gooeyness, the gang were tanked up on love vibes and ready to take down the Spider Monster at Starcourt Mall.

Every Breath You Take, The Police (1983)

■ Growing up is hard. Feelings are weird. Dancing is even harder, which is why the right song at the right time can shunt things along. When this song came on at The Snow Ball, it gave Lucas and Max the nudge they needed to move beyond just being friends. When El and Mike heard it, they took similar steps: left-right-left, then Mike finally got the courage to show El why they weren't like brother and sister.

Nancy digs Blondie. Blondie were a massive New Wave band. Jonathan loves New Wave music – so that's pretty atomic.

Running Up that Hill, Kate Bush (1985)

■ What witchcraft was this? The music of Kate Bush proved so powerful that it worked as a protective spell for Max when she entered Vecna's Mind Lair. It was her lifeline back to the real world, it was her comfort, her connection to love and the love of life. Kate's voice was as soothing as the beat was energising and words powerful.

Jim Hopper is a sucker for Jim Croce, especially his song, 'You Don't Mess Around with Jim,' which is obviously an anthem of empowerment for the police chief.

Master of Puppets, Metallica (1986)

■ Eddie Munson lures the Demobats away from Vecna's lair by playing: "the most metal concert ever." That means shredding his guitar to one of Metallica's most righteous head-bangers, 'Master of Puppets'. In this moment Eddie himself became the puppet master – making the dimbobats do exactly as he wished.

Billy and Eddie were both metalheads who loved Metallica. Shame they never met. Bigger shame they're both dead.

"I MADE YOU A NEW MIXTAPE. I THINK THERE'S SOME STUFF ON THERE YOU REALLY MIGHT LIKE."

JONATHAN

When Will gets back from the Upside Down, Jonathan gives Will a new mixtape of his favourite bands. While we don't know the exact track listing, evidence suggests it would include tracks from bands like these:

JONATHAN'S MIXTAPE OF 'REAL' MUSIC FOR WILL

PLAY VERY LOUD!

SIDE A

1. THE CLASH
2. TALKING HEADS
3. DAVID BOWIE
4. SHOCK THERAPY
5. PSYCHEDELIC FURS
6. SWING SET
7. RAMONES
8. HAND IN GLOVE

SIDE B

1. JOY DIVISION
2. JEFFERSON AIRPLANE
3. SMART REMARKS
4. DEVO
5. OINGO BOINGO
6. ROY ORBISON
7. TELEVISION
8. BLONDIE

TRAINING TEST

CRACK THE CODE

with Robin and Nancy

Investigation queens, Nancy and Robin are stuck; there are too many messages to decode. Help them to unscramble the anagrams relating to the nightmare happenings in Hawkins.

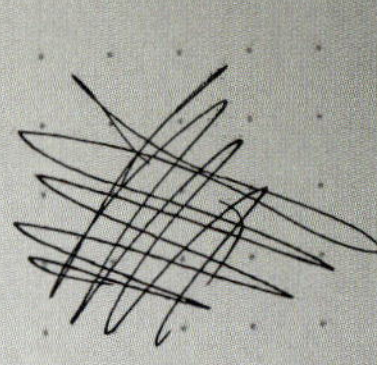

1. LIFE TRIERS (one word)
Clue: Earthy snack for mindless copycats.

_ _ _ _ _ _ _ _ _ _

2. MOLLUSC TARTAR (two words)
Clue: Find Eleven there, shopping.

_ _ _ _ _ _ _ _ _   _ _ _ _

3. MINK PUP (one word)
Clue: Seasonal coffee, pie, soup and spice.

_ _ _ _ _ _ _

4. AGO CHIC (one word)
Clue: Find Eleven there, escaping.

_ _ _ _ _ _ _

5. ANGST ME (one word)
Clue: Joyce can't make them stick.

_ _ _ _ _ _ _

6. DEAMONS THROWS (two words)
Clue: Outline of Will's biggest foe.

_ _ _ _ _ _   _ _ _ _ _ _ _

7. CAPTOR JENNI (two words)
Clue: Find Eleven there, submerged.

_ _ _ _   _ _ _ _ _ _ _

8. CELERY HERN (two words)
Clue: Bad boy.

_ _ _ _ _   _ _ _ _ _

9. BILL CHEERFUL (two words)
Clue: Not satanic D&D fans.

_ _ _ _ _ _ _ _   _ _ _ _

10. ARMANI KINO (two words)
Clue: Find Eleven there, on wheels.

_ _ _ _ _ _ _ _ _ _

ANSWERS ON PAGE 119

TRAINING TEST

DEMOBAT ATTACK!

Count the number of demobats and save Eddie from a fate worse than Phil Collins.

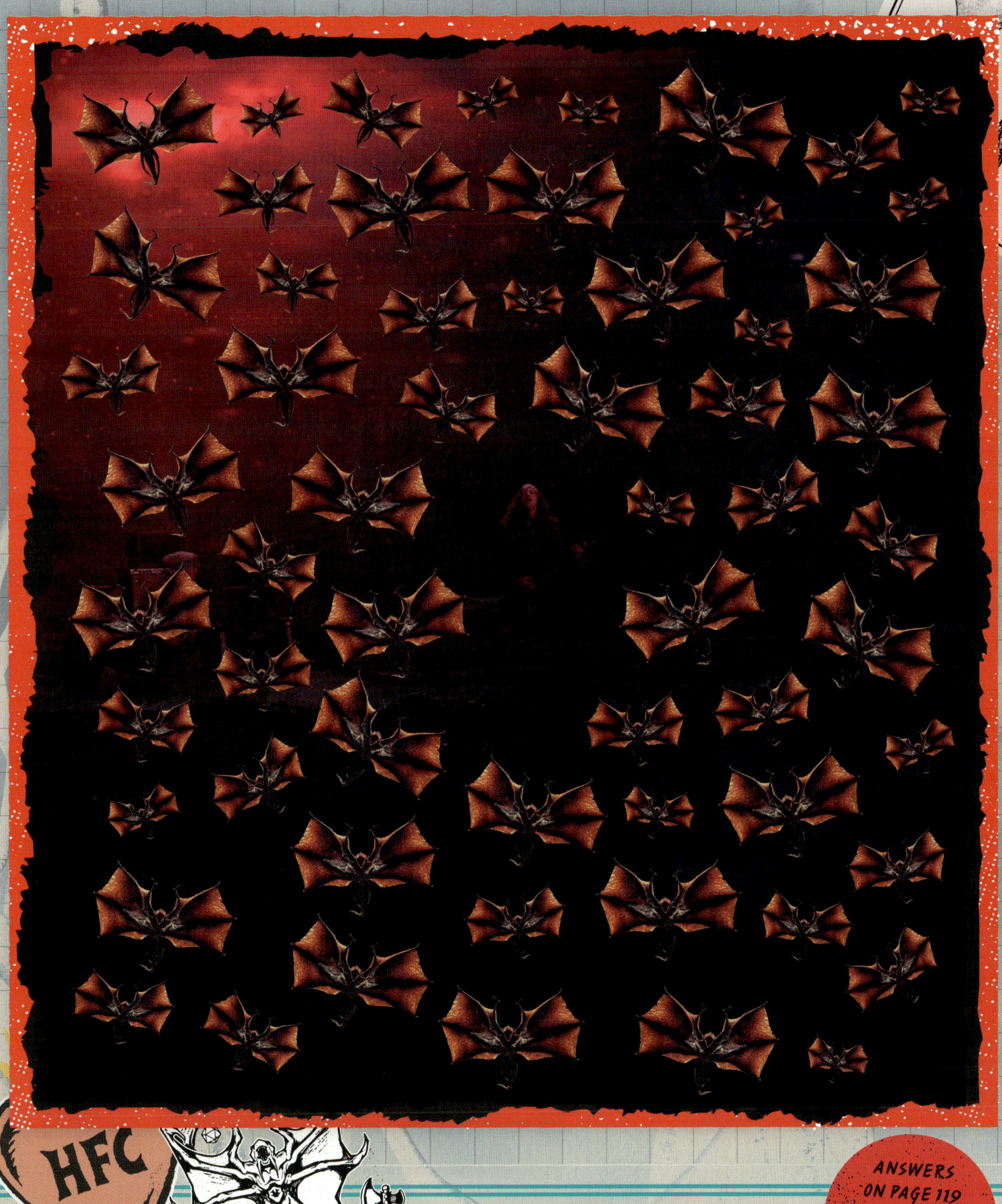

ANSWERS ON PAGE 119

HEROICS IN 1986

'86 ... this is my year,' said Eddie Munson, hopefully. But it was not to be. This was the hardest battle yet. How did the plucky Hawkins crew survive? By splitting up and in some cases, not actually surviving. Sob!

■ The D&D gang of four: 'The Party', expanded to include some older boys, including the charismatic misfit Eddie Munson. The group was called Hellfire Club. Playing Dungeons & Dragons with Eddie as Dungeon Master, they encountered the game's dark wizard, Lord Vecna, so naturally, when they meet an evil entity in the Upside Down they name him 'Vecna.' Warning – the dude is a rotten egg.

■ Vecna puts a curse on a series of teenagers that kills them and opens portals to his dark underworld. One of those teenagers is Max, but she had a way to fight him. The glorious music of Kate Bush.

■ As cool as Kate Bush is, she couldn't help Max fight Vecna alone. Eleven would be the perfect 'weapon,' but she'd lost her powers. Luckily, Dr Brenner and Dr Owens had created a machine they called Nina, designed to bring El's powers back through a process of reliving her traumatic time in 1979 at Hawkins Lab.

■ Eleven eventually remembers everything that happened to her at Hawkins Lab, including the discovery that her 'friend' Henry was in fact subject 001, and Vecna himself, who she'd banished to the Upside Down after he murdered everyone. Such a rotten egg.

■ The gang weapon-up to kill Vecna before he kills Max. They plan to go through one of the portals to the Upside Down and end him when he's distracted.

■ Will, Mike and Jonathan team up with Jonathan's new mate Argyle to rescue El from from her desert fortress.

■ Meanwhile, Joyce is on a rescue mission of her own. Getting Hopper out of the Russian prison where he's being made to fight a Demogorgon. Yeah, it's complicated.

■ With the help of Lucas and Erica, Max sets herself up as bait in Vecna's old house. She switches off her 'protector,' Kate Bush and brazenly asks lord no-nose: "Do you want me or not?" Spoiler. He wants her!

■ Nancy, Robin and Steve enter the Creel House in the Upside Down and Vecna is there, as expected, but the deadly network of tentacles trap them. Luckily, Joyce and Hopper kill a bunch of Demo-creatures in Russia, which weakens the hive mind and allows the kids to escape.

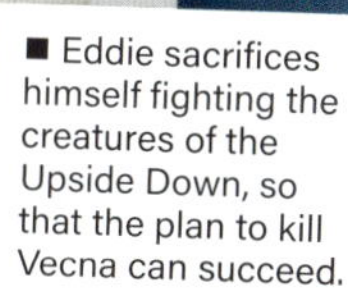

■ Eddie sacrifices himself fighting the creatures of the Upside Down, so that the plan to kill Vecna can succeed.

■ Free from Project Nina, Eleven 'piggybacks' from a pizza dough freezer into Max's mind to help her remotely fight Vecna.

■ It's not entirely successful. In his Mind Lair, Vecna kills Max and opens his final portal. Eleven strikes back, pinning Vecna to one of his own corpse trees. "This is only the beginning" he seethes, as Steve sets fire to him IRL and Nancy blasts him out of the window.

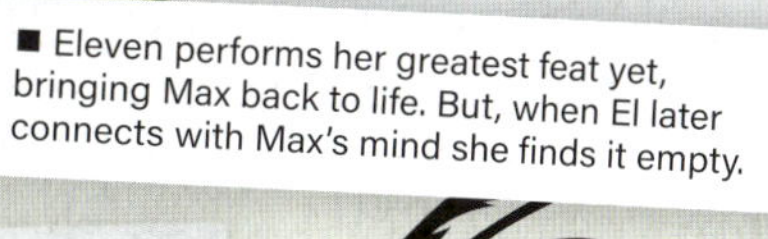

■ Eleven performs her greatest feat yet, bringing Max back to life. But, when El later connects with Max's mind she finds it empty.

BAD IDEA!

Eddie didn't need to lure the Demobats away from Dustin, and fight them so majestically, did he? DID HE?

■ There is no more information available at this time, but Vecna did not die from his window-fall and annoyingly he was right: the battle has only just begun.

RAD IDEA!

Putting El in a makeshift isolation tank to help Max, was a genius idea that saved her life – or at least restarted it – we think.

"Nina is not a small woman. Ignore Argyle."

CLOSE UP ON ...

THE NINA PROJECT

A war was coming with no weapons to fight it. Eleven had to become that weapon. And so she returned to the 'care' of her 'Papa' to become bitchin' again.

DID YOU KNOW ...

THE NINA PROJECT WAS NAMED AFTER THE 1786 OPERA, 'NINA', BY NICOLAS DALAYRAC. IN THE OPERA, NINA IS SO TRAUMATISED BY THE DEATH OF HER LOVER THAT SHE FORGETS HE EVER DIED, REPRESSING THE UNHAPPY MEMORY, WHICH IS PRETTY MUCH WHAT ELEVEN DID – EXCEPT SHE BLOCKED OUT THE DEATHS OF EVERYONE AT THE LAB.

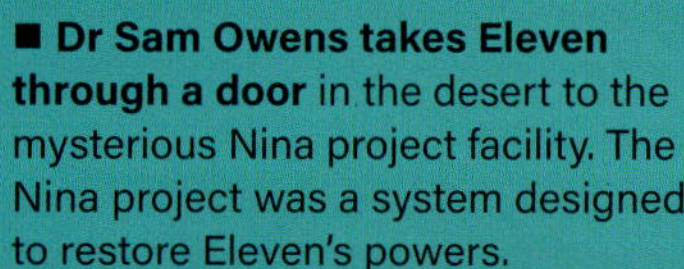

■ **Dr Sam Owens takes Eleven through a door** in the desert to the mysterious Nina project facility. The Nina project was a system designed to restore Eleven's powers.

■ Eleven was prepared to work with non-creep Dr Owens, but **seeing that Dr Brenner, her 'Papa', was involved gave Eleven second thoughts**. Could she trust him? No of course not, but she did it anyway.

"You're home."
Brenner

■ Eleven missed having her powers, she missed not being able to defend herself against bullies and she genuinely wanted to help save her friends and Hawkins. But she also feared that without her powers she was too boring for Mike. Basically, she wanted to be the superhero people thought she was. **That's why she agreed to be 'experimented' on again.**

■ **Dr Brenner plans to wire Eleven up to the past** with a meticulous library of surveillance videos, so that her brain believes that she's actually there again. The theory is that as she discovers her powers in the past, they will return to her in the present.

■ **Eleven wears a cap covered in electrodes,** connecting her brain to the computer systems, so that Brenner and Owens can monitor her responses.

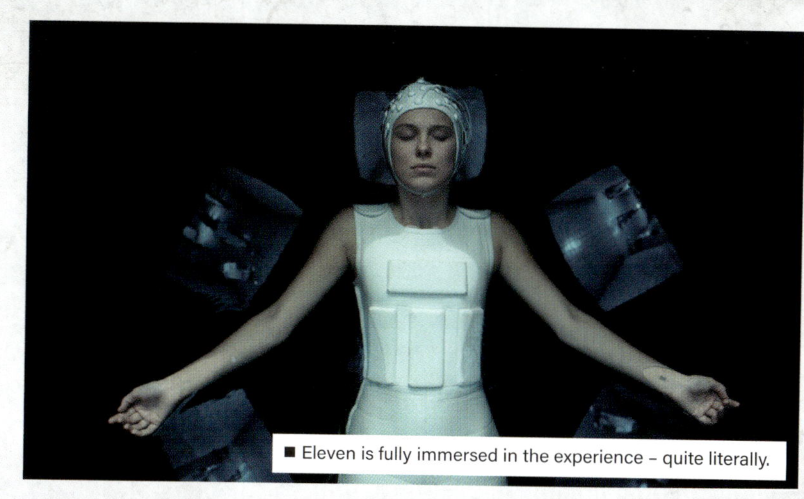

■ Eleven is fully immersed in the experience – quite literally.

■ **El instantly found herself back in the Hawkins Lab** and it was weird as hell. She was scared and her instinct was to run, but after some serious déjà vu she adjusted to the process and began to find out what had gone on there with 001, 002 etc ...

"Someone's a sleepyhead this morning."

Henry

■ The road to discovery wasn't easy. Eleven blocked out these painful memories for a reason. She feared being the monster and when she broke out of the machine, she wanted OUT altogether, **taking out guards with her re-emerging powers**. Thankfully she calmed down.

■ Eleven knew she had to soldier on, **but the process of remembering took its toll**. She experienced being bullied all over again, something she had actually just suffered in Lenora, California – and that was before she discovered what Henry did and what she did to stop him.

■ Long-story-short: the project worked. It nearly killed her, but Eleven's powers returned. She proved it to everyone by **lifting the massive Nina cylinder thingy.**

■ Eleven was finally ready to take on Vecna. Except she wasn't really ready at all. No one is ever ready for that.

OMG Gnarly!

TERROR AT THE ROLLER RINK

Eleven has faced much worse than a bunch of snarky teens on wheels, but when their leader, Angela, went in for the kill, Eleven said – not today blondie!

RINK-O-MANIA ROLLER S

22 MARCH 1986
2.36PM

Daytime at the roller disco. Sounds like fun. And it might've been. El and Mike were reunited. The music was banging out Tarzan Boy by Baltimora. Good times. Until the boys took a breather from the 8-wheel life and left El to fend for herself ...

■ Reunited and it feels so good. But not for gooseberry-in-the-middle Will.

■ William Byers rolls alone – sob.

The roller-skating girls of Eleven's new hometown crowded around shouting a dizzying number of insults:

"Freak!" "Loser!"
"Go home!"

Eleven began to wobble. She was crushed. Not even Lucas at his most sceptical was this cruel. She covered her ears to try and block out the bleating jibes. Mike pleaded with the DJ to shut the music off. But he wouldn't listen.

The more upset Eleven became, the happier the bullies were. They joined hands forming a circle around her, trapping her like a caged animal. Unfortunately, this was a feeling she was familiar with.

Finally, the music stopped and a dude rolls up and throws a chocolate shake in El's face.

"WIPEOUT" the DJ yelled, not helping at all.

RINK-O-MANIA ROLLERSKATING

El rolled backwards, collapsing on the roller rink as the crowd howled with laughter, pointing and clapping like her humiliation was the best thing to ever happen to Lenora Hills. What a dump.

Mike and Will watched with horror, frozen, not sure what to do. Not sure what Eleven would do. They had seen her retaliate before. Could she control herself? Was that even possible?

With her prey on the ground, Angela rolled round for the last word. "Didn't you see the sign, dummy. No food or drinks on the rink."

It was a rubbish joke, and El didn't find it funny either.

RINK -O- MANIA

Ok, so Angela's last-last word came a bit later. Eleven had managed to hold in her rage, get up and take off her skates – all without psychically snapping Angela's neck or making the mean girl pee herself. But, bullies gotta bully and so stupid Angela, not aware of who she was messing with, marched up to El to make fun of her all over again – this time for being an orphan. Well, that did it; Eleven snapped!

As Angela walked away triumphant and villainous, El picked up a roller skate and smashed it into her face. Thwack! Blood everywhere. Worst disco ever.

Violence is never the answer, but at least she hadn't used her powers, so when she was carted off to the police station she was assumed to be just another regular-degular teenage tearaway.

ELEVEN

YOUR NUMBER IS UP!

Is the math, mathing? Are there patterns in the numbers? One day it might all make sense.

5'6

■ Eleven's height when she gets arrested by Lenora Hills PD.

10

■ The number of hours The Party spent playing D&D on the night of Will's disappearance.

Will Byers' stats when he was possessed by the Mind Flayer:

220BPM

■ Will's heart rate.

106°C

■ Will's temperature

1983

■ The year the Upside Down appears to be frozen at.

134

■ The issue of The Uncanny X-Men that Will raced Dustin for.

5★

■ Dustin refers to the Demogorgon as Vecna's 5-star General.

18

■ Number of known child subjects in the Hawkins Lab experiments.

20

■ The number of sides on a D20 D&D die.

3

■ The number of inches Eleven's door needs to be left ajar.

3.15PM

■ The time El and Will first agreed to meet by the powerlines behind his house.

7-11

■ Where Alexei picked up his cherry Slurpee.

450

■ The number of volts used to fry Terry Ives' brain.

6.62607004

■ Planck's constant, the password as suggested by Dusty's Suzie-poo.

$3.50

■ The amount of cash Mike went shopping with to get Eleven a gift at the mall.

PCE 235

■ The numberplate on Billy's Camaro.

$40,000

■ The amount requested for Jim Hopper's ransom from the Russian prison.

TELEPHONE BOOK

001-618-625-8313
THE NUMBER TO SEND A TIP-OFF TO MURRAY BAUMAN IN HIS LAIR.

001-805-45-PIZZA (74992)
ORDER A SURFER BOY PIZZA, BROCHACHO.

001-202-968-6161
DO NOT DIAL THE NUMBER FOR THE NINA PROJECT HQ. THESE GUYS ARE SCARY. THEY WILL FIND YOU.

*****Do not call these numbers** without the permission of an adult. They are real numbers that will be answered.***

352

■ The number of days Mike and El went without seeing each other, 1983-1984.

185

■ The number of days Mike and El went without seeing each other 1985-1986.

SCORES

751,300 - MADMAX
650,990 - DUSTIN
641,183 - LUCAS

MR CLARKE'S SCIENCE LESSON

Take a moment to open a few curiosity doors and you'll quickly discover that many of the 'unreal' happenings are actually explainable by science.

FLOATATION TANKS

Floating in warm, salt water in a sensory deprivation tank, like the one Eleven uses, is not uncommon as a form of physical therapy. Today the practise is referred to as 'Reduced or Restricted Environmental Stimulation Therapy'. It might sound a bit scary, but some people who use them for conditions such as depression, anxiety and pain, find that their symptoms much improved after time in the tank. You can book sessions for around £50.

HIVE MINDS

Every living thing in the Upside Down seems to be connected. The beings, from the icky vines, to the Demodogs and the Mind Flayer all seem to operate as one single entity. This has been observed in real-world forests, where trees and plants communicate with each other through signals both in the air and underground in their root systems.

MAGNETS

There's a theory that magnets are so good at defying the rather weedy force of gravity we experience on Earth because gravity is being weakened by the pull across other dimensions. That's a pretty big flex, but if true it explains the magnetic interference witnessed first-hand by Joyce Byers.

"Science is neat, but I'm afraid it's not very forgiving."

Scott Clarke

OTHER WORLDS

The acrobat and the flea. In a metaphor for other dimensions Mr Clarke explained that an acrobat on a tightrope can only walk forwards and backwards on the top of the rope, but that a flea can walk all around it, sideways and – even underneath. The flea can travel to places the human cannot. This metaphor is similar to El's other-side-of-the-board analogy. Mr Clarke used a folded paper plate.

"OUR OFFICE IS PROUD TO CONTINUE TO FUND CUTTING EDGE RESEARCH IN DIVERSE TOPICS IN HIGH ENERGY PHYSICS."

"THIS RESEARCH WILL ALLOW US TO MAKE NEW ADVANCEMENTS IN OUR UNDERSTANDING OF THE UNIVERSE."

SPOKESPERSON FOR THE UNITED STATES DEPARTMENT OF ENERGY.

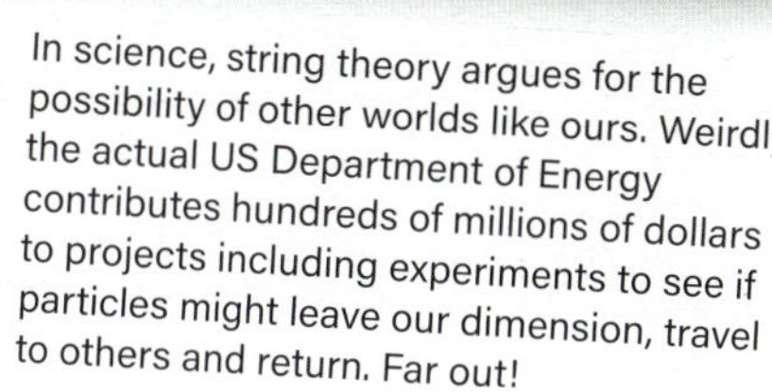

In science, string theory argues for the possibility of other worlds like ours. Weirdly, the actual US Department of Energy contributes hundreds of millions of dollars to projects including experiments to see if particles might leave our dimension, travel to others and return. Far out!

MIND CONTROL

Did you know that neuroscientists can map various behaviours we make by looking at what the brain is doing when we make that movement? Once we know the pathways in the brain that cause a certain thing, science can make that thing happen by manipulating the brain – brain control. This is most clearly shown through the way a robotic arm works. Certain thoughts make the arm do certain things. Bearing that in mind, Will or Billy could be seen as the robotic arm of the Mind Flayer.

SLIME MOULDS

If you think the blobby creature that consumed all the rats and some of the inhabitants of Hawkins seems too unbelievable to be true, then take a look at slime mould. Slime mould can exist as single-cell individual organisms consuming bacteria in the soil, but when resources are scarce, they join up to become a larger more powerful being. This is literally what's happening with the flesh thralls in the Steel Works. To make things even freakier, if you put slime mould in a maze it will find the food, while avoiding any strong light source, which it actively dislikes. Sound familiar?

TRAINING TEST

REWIND

Have you been paying attention?Are you going to be helpful in the next fight for Hawkins? Tell Florence everything and she'll file the report with Chief Hopper.

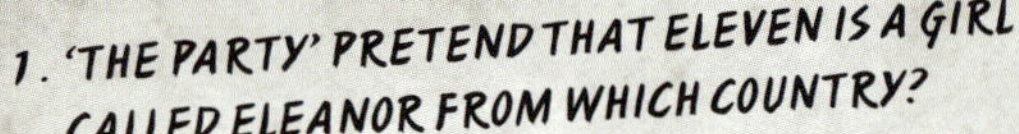

1. 'THE PARTY' PRETEND THAT ELEVEN IS A GIRL CALLED ELEANOR FROM WHICH COUNTRY?

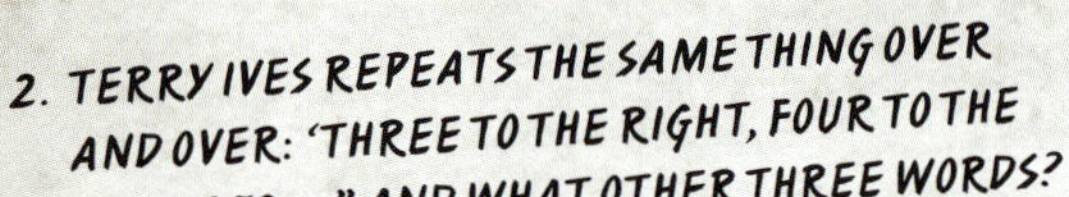

2. TERRY IVES REPEATS THE SAME THING OVER AND OVER: 'THREE TO THE RIGHT, FOUR TO THE LEFT, 450...' AND WHAT OTHER THREE WORDS?

3. WHICH INSECT DOES MR CLARKE SAY CAN WALK ALL THE WAY AROUND A TIGHTROPE IN HIS METAPHOR FOR A CREATURE THAN CAN TRAVEL BETWEEN DIMENSIONS.

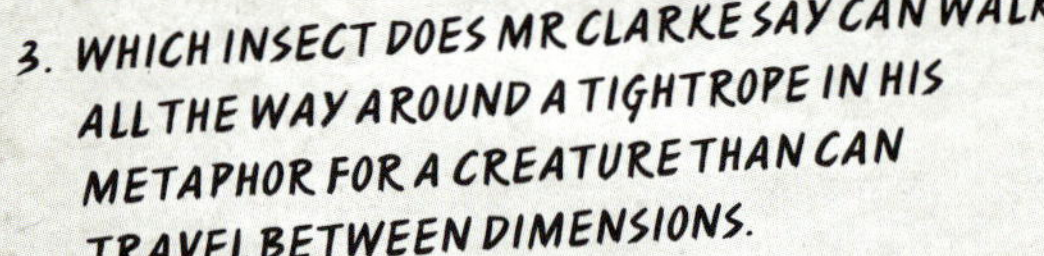

4. WHAT ARE EGGOS? HINT: EL'S FAVOURITE FOOD.

5. WHO ARE FROG FACE AND TOOTHLESS?

6. HOW MANY FLESH-FLAP 'PETALS' DOES THE DEMOGORGON'S FLOWER-FACE OPEN INTO?

7. WHAT FLAVOUR SLURPEE DOES ALEXEI REALLY, REALLY, REALLY WANT?

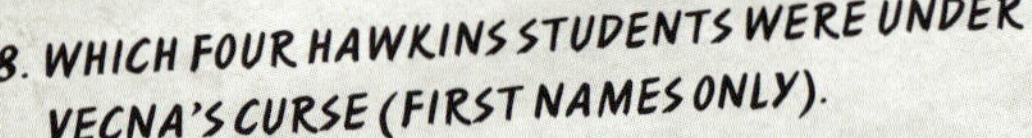

8. WHICH FOUR HAWKINS STUDENTS WERE UNDER VECNA'S CURSE (FIRST NAMES ONLY).

9. KALI WAS THE GIRL WHO ESCAPED HAWKINS LAB: WHAT WAS HER SUBJECT NUMBER?

10. WHERE DID DUSTIN MEET SUZIE?

11. WHICH THREE LANGUAGES DOES ROBIN SAY SHE CAN SPEAK?

12. AT WHICH RESTAURANT WERE HOPPER AND JOYCE SUPPOSED TO HAVE THEIR FIRST DATE?

13. WILL HAS A DEN IN THE WOODS, WHAT IS IT CALLED?

14. WHAT IS STEVE HARINGTON'S NICKNAME?

15. WHAT DATE DOES THE FAYRE TAKE PLACE?

16. DART ENJOYS WHICH AMERICAN CANDY BAR?

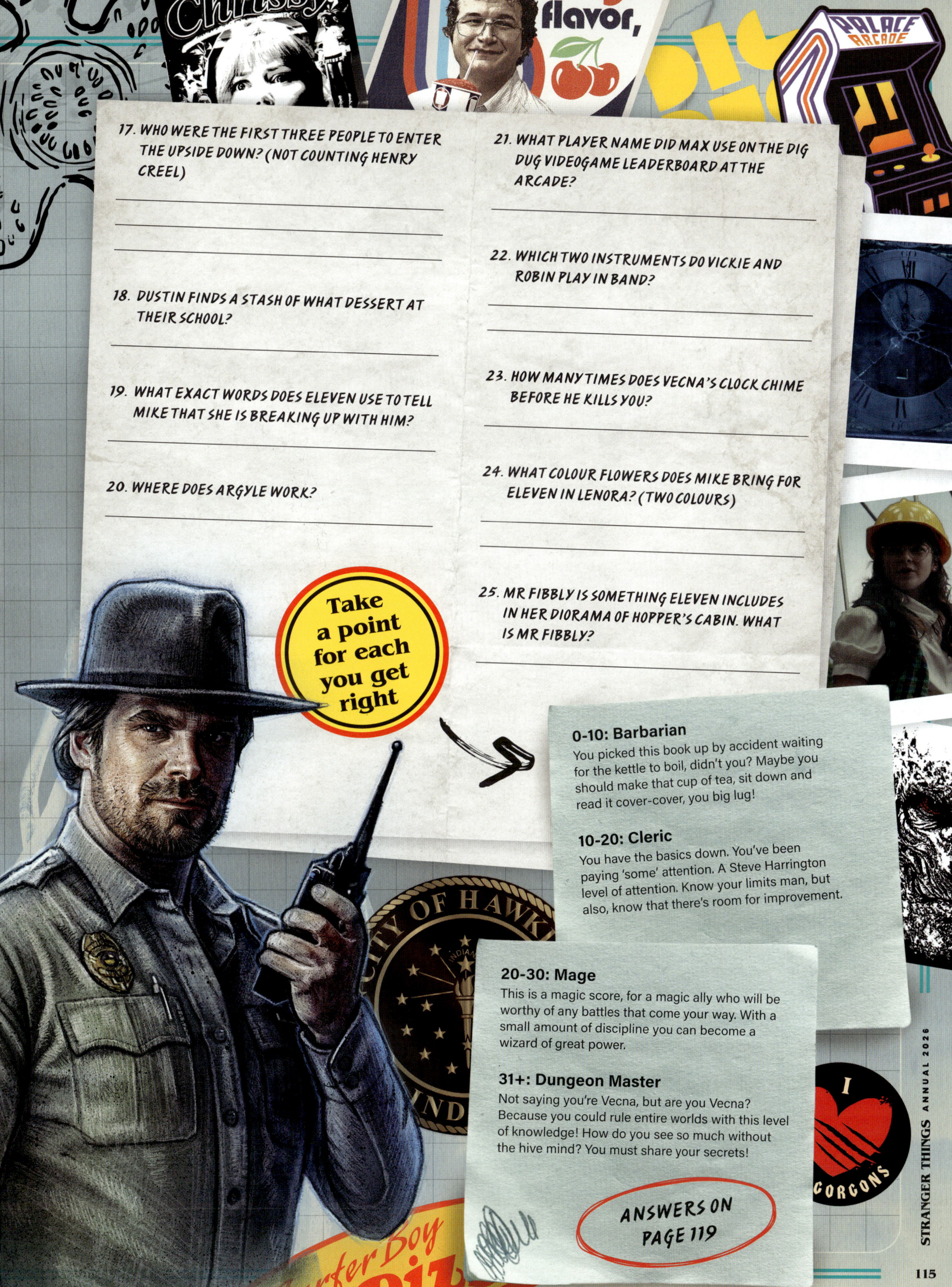

17. WHO WERE THE FIRST THREE PEOPLE TO ENTER THE UPSIDE DOWN? (NOT COUNTING HENRY CREEL)

18. DUSTIN FINDS A STASH OF WHAT DESSERT AT THEIR SCHOOL?

19. WHAT EXACT WORDS DOES ELEVEN USE TO TELL MIKE THAT SHE IS BREAKING UP WITH HIM?

20. WHERE DOES ARGYLE WORK?

21. WHAT PLAYER NAME DID MAX USE ON THE DIG DUG VIDEOGAME LEADERBOARD AT THE ARCADE?

22. WHICH TWO INSTRUMENTS DO VICKIE AND ROBIN PLAY IN BAND?

23. HOW MANY TIMES DOES VECNA'S CLOCK CHIME BEFORE HE KILLS YOU?

24. WHAT COLOUR FLOWERS DOES MIKE BRING FOR ELEVEN IN LENORA? (TWO COLOURS)

25. MR FIBBLY IS SOMETHING ELEVEN INCLUDES IN HER DIORAMA OF HOPPER'S CABIN. WHAT IS MR FIBBLY?

Take a point for each you get right

0-10: Barbarian
You picked this book up by accident waiting for the kettle to boil, didn't you? Maybe you should make that cup of tea, sit down and read it cover-cover, you big lug!

10-20: Cleric
You have the basics down. You've been paying 'some' attention. A Steve Harrington level of attention. Know your limits man, but also, know that there's room for improvement.

20-30: Mage
This is a magic score, for a magic ally who will be worthy of any battles that come your way. With a small amount of discipline you can become a wizard of great power.

31+: Dungeon Master
Not saying you're Vecna, but are you Vecna? Because you could rule entire worlds with this level of knowledge! How do you see so much without the hive mind? You must share your secrets!

ANSWERS ON PAGE 119

WHAT'S NEXT?

THE NEXT BATTLE IS ALREADY HERE

The world is about to experience a monster makeover of the most awful magnitude, and we're not talking wet-look gel and goth amounts of eyeliner.

Together again

■ After defeating Vecna, the gang had some heartfelt reunions, and it was very necessary. But before anyone could even relax, Will felt his neck prickle, in that second he knew that they hadn't won – not yet. The game was far from finished. They had one last campaign to go.

Is it snowing?

■ The skies filled with Upside Down particles, that little Holly mistook for snow, but there was no mistaking the swirling smoke rising from cracks in the earth.

The gates are open

■ The gang went to explore, to witness what was happening to their beloved town. Vecna's four gates had split the place apart and it had already begun to die.

Good vs Evil

■ Eleven has her powers now. She's fought Vecna and she knows what she's up against. We have to put our faith in the fact that she can save us, that her friends can save us. If not we're all puppy food for the Demodogs.

LEAVING
HAWKINS
COME AGAIN SOON

TRAINING TEST COMPLETE

ANSWERS

Pages 14-15: U R Here

1. Hawkins High School
2. The Hawkins Post
3. Benny's Burgers
4. Castle Byers
5. Creel House
6. Starcourt Mall
7. Hawkins Community Pool
8. Hawkins Middle School
9. Palace Arcade
10. Hawkins National Laboratory

Page 21: Psychic Wordsearch

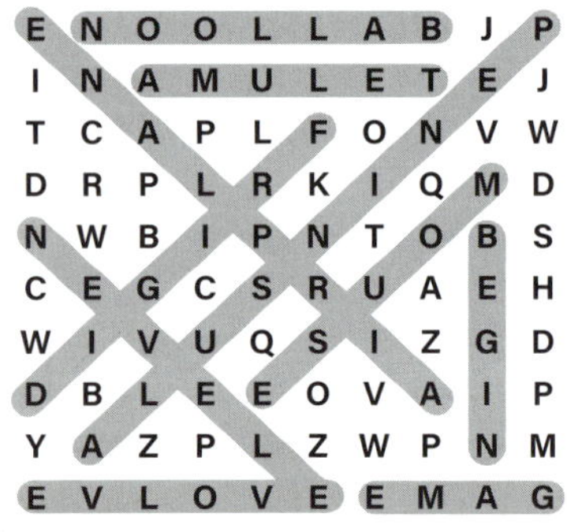

Pages 30-31: Guess who in Hawkins!

1. Nancy
2. Steve
3. Demogorgon
4. Hopper
5. Vecna
6. Erica
7. Eleven
8. Dr Brenner
9. Lucas
10. Fred
11. Henry

Page 52: Lookout with Lucas

1. Steve: Go Say Hi.
2. Dustin and Dart: Sit and Wait.
3. Grigori: Run Away.
4. Hawkins Power and Light: Sit and Wait.
5. Max: Go Say Hi
6. Hospital monster: Run Away.

Pages 42-43: Escape from Hawkins Lab

Page 53: Spot the difference

Page 60: Search and destroy

Page 76: Who said it?

Nancy: H – "Nobody deviates from the plan, no matter what."

Mike: C – "If anyone asks where I am, I've left the country."

Max: F – "And I like talking with you, stalker."

Lucas: B – "We have a lot of rules in our party, but the most important is, 'Friends don't lie.'"

Eddie: J – "Chrissy, wake up. I don't like this, Chrissy. Wake up!"

Will: A – "Run!"

Erica: I – "Nerd."

Jonathan: D – "I made you a new mixtape."

Argyle: G – "Who would I tell? You're my only friend, Jonathan."

Eleven: E – "What is, friend?"